SOUTHCENTRAL ALASKA

A COMPREHENSIVE GUIDE TO HIKING & CANOEING TRAILS & PUBLIC-USE CABINS

ALAN JUBENVILLE

HUNTER
PUBLISHING

HUNTER PUBLISHING, INC.
130 Campus Drive
Edison NJ 08818-7816, USA
Tel (908) 225 1900; Fax (908) 417 0482
E-mail hunterpub@emi.net
www.hunterpublishing.com

1220 Nicholson Road
Newmarket, Ontario L3Y 7V1, CANADA
Tel (800) 399 6858; Fax (800) 363 2665

ISBN 1-55650-781-X

© 1997 Hunter Publishing

Maps by Scott Penwell
Cover photo by Bob Krist, Leo de Wys
all others by author unless noted otherwise.

SOUTHCENTRAL ALASKA

A COMPREHENSIVE GUIDE TO HIKING & CANOEING TRAILS & PUBLIC-USE CABINS

ALASKA: THE LAND OF HIKING

Alaska is viewed as the last frontier, the last oasis of wilderness, a hiker's paradise. This book is for those who want to access these pristine landscapes via trail. It is my hope that you find this book as interesting and exciting in planning your own adventures as it was for me compiling, verifying, and savoring each tiny piece of the puzzle.

The purpose of the book is to give information about trails that are accessed by existing transportation systems. Aside from roads, which form the core of the transportation system, Alaska also has the marine highway in Southeast and Southcentral, allowing additional access to even more trails. This book focuses on summer and fall hiking opportunities, but there are many other trails strictly open to cross-country skiers, ORV drivers and snowmobilers in winter. Simply contact the controlling agency for information. The book attempts to be as comprehensive as possible, covering everything from the half-mile interpretive trail focusing on bog ecology to the 30-mile wilderness mountain trail. After an initial comprehensive study of all trails in the region, some trails were omitted from the guide for various reasons – because they crossed private lands, were not adequately maintained, or were not managed for the hiker.

Choosing the "right" trail can mean many things to the same person. It can be a spontaneous decision to take an afternoon out of doors. Or, it can be a week-long trip into the high country to relax and take pictures of wildflowers or wildlife. It might be an adventurous stay in a public cabin, with walks radiating out to points of interest each day. In any case, this book should give you sufficient information for the stand-alone trip where hiking is the primary activity, as well as a trip where hiking simply gets you to your destination, such as a lake or public cabin.

Helping to choose the "right" setting for your hiking adventure is also important. There are many varied geological and ecological environments. Some are very exciting and attractive; others are less stimulating. Still others are not very appealing at all. That said, most designated trails typically lead through and to some of the most stunning natural areas in the state. Trail profiles throughout this book will give you an idea of the landscape and features you might encounter en route. Potential constraints on trail usage, such as season, presence of bears, steepness of the trail, etc., are also taken into consideration.

Safety is a constant concern when travelling these spectacular routes. If a trail ends above timberline and it is possible to continue your hike, this portion of the route is only recommended where it is easily identifiable on the ground. There are a few trails included here which are primarily used by ORV drivers. Those trails are the best access into unique landscapes, and thus deserve a place in this book. In some cases, the trails are poorly maintained. If the trail is safe and passable, it is listed in the book and local conditions are noted, but you should always check with local authorities about oncoming weather patterns. Facilities along each trail are also shown, including public-use cabins.

Contact the responsible agency before venturing out. There is no good substitute for current, accurate information.

Trails are a great way to enjoy Alaska. *Bonne chance!*

HOW TO USE THIS BOOK

To find the beginning of a trail, I have included directions – typically with a milepost number along the main road system. Keep in mind that roads have been periodically rerouted such that a milepost may be missing or not reflect the present mileage along the route. But most mileposts are in place, and the major features along the road are given to avoid confusion. Even if mileposts are missing, you should still be able to find the trailhead. Local addresses and telephone numbers of the responsible agencies are provided so you can seek specific local conditions prior to your departure.

The *Introduction* deals with planning your hiking adventure. The *Basics* chapter focuses on activities while out on the trail. The remaining chapters describe the individual trails by region.

WE LOVE TO GET MAIL

Hunter Publishing is dedicated to providing the most up-to-date travel guides available. Please let us know of any omissions, corrections or changes in trail conditions so that they may be incorporated into future editions of this book. Your recommendations are appreciated. We are also keen to hear of your travel experiences while in Alaska. Please address all communication to:

Alan Jubenville
P.O. Box 82970
Fairbanks, AK 99708-2970

DEDICATION

This book is dedicated to a friend who has long
been my inspiration. He encouraged me to be
what I wanted to be, to pursue the ideas that
were important to me, and to share with others
the richness of life that I found along the way.
That friend was my father, Wayne Jubenville.

CONTENTS

MAPS

INTRODUCTION

TRIP PLANNING

Planning your hiking adventure requires more thought than when camping at an auto campground or boat fishing at your favorite lake. First, you have to take your camp with you. There are no opportunities to purchase forgotten food or equipment once you are on the trail. One piece of missing equipment can be life-threatening – a stove, a match or sleeping bag. Second, you have to keep food, equipment and supplies within the volume limits of your pack and its weight must be no more than you can carry. Lastly, you want to enjoy the trip and be able to handle most contingencies as they arise. This means not only the 10-day trek into the mountains, but also the two-hour family hike to a lake.

It is not only important to have the right food, clothing and equipment, but also to prepare yourself mentally – to arrive at your destination in one piece, enjoy your activities while there and return safely, handling everything that comes your way without too big a fuss. *The Basics* chapter on page 29 focuses on these aspects, including those unique to Alaska.

PREPARING FOR YOUR ALASKAN HIKING EXPERIENCE

Alaska is probably similar to other places you have hiked; however, there are some obvious differences – grizzly bears, glaciers, weather patterns and cold silty streams. Without good preparation, you may run into difficult conditions that you are unprepared to deal with. You can't just wait until they occur; you must take with you the proper equipment and knowledge. Some information may seem redundant for the advanced traveler, but all of it is essential in preparing for your Alaskan adventure.

I can guarantee you that, if you are fully prepared, you will experience some of the most spectacular country Alaska has to offer. You will see beautiful mountain peaks, picturesque lakes, alpine wildflowers, unusual wildlife, fantastic sunsets (you may have to stay up late to see them!) and panoramas that never seem to end. Along the trails you are bound to meet some interesting people who share your enthusiasm for the natural beauty that abounds in this region. Be courteous to others, minimizing your impact on their experiences, and hope they do the same.

An eco-conscious traveler will bring back vivid memories and photographs, leaving only footprints easily erased by the next rainstorm. By minimizing your impact, these delicate areas will remain intact for your return visit and for generations yet to be born.

The glacial carved landscape of Southcentral Alaska.

THE BASICS OF YOUR TRIP

Making the right decisions at the planning stage will maximize your enjoyment of the great outdoors. In this land, making the wrong decision can also place you in a life-threatening situation. Dealing with nature's hazards is crucial. It is the total experience that you are planning; thus, every element of your trip should be considered in the planning process.

Hiking for most people is not an end in itself, but a means to an end. For some, it may be a lazy afternoon above timberline picking berries, photographing wildflowers, talking to the pikas, or wandering with the sheep and goats. Others may prefer a long-distance overnight trip to a specific destination point, such as a mountain lake, a breathtaking shoreline or a beautiful hidden cove to do their "thing," be it photographing wildlife, catching delicious grayling for supper, or just enjoying the roar of the calving glacier. Still others may prefer to base themselves at a public-use cabin and explore from there on short day trips. Whatever choice is made, each and every one of these excursions requires some planning. Obviously, the more lengthy trips require more attention to details because of the logistics involved, but never, never think that the short trips do not require advance thought. The time spent putting together your gear, food and emergency provisions will pay off even on the shortest hike. If for no other reason than just knowing you have the situation well in hand, planning is a necessary part of any Alaskan vacation.

GETTING SUFFICIENT INFORMATION

The information in this book will help with your initial preparations. It will give you many trail options, detailing their specific attributes — distance from your home, available activities, quality of the landscape, difficulty in travel and so on. Opportunities for hiking in Southcentral abound, but often information is not available. With this book and by contacting the managing agency *before your trip*, you will have new alternatives to consider before narrowing them down to two or three choices and then studying those in greater detail.

Choices can be made, reviewed or changed in order to arrive at the best itinerary for you. It gives time for you and your group to look forward to the upcoming hiking experience, allowing for ample preparation time and improving the outcome.

PROPER MAPS

Most of the trails presented in the book are actively managed by a public agency. Typically, each agency will put together specific information on a given trail, perhaps even a trail map. A map can be especially helpful, particularly if it has contours, vegetation, natural features such as rivers and mountain peaks, and cultural features, such as roads, buildings and trails.

The **U.S. Geological Survey** offers such maps in 1:63,360 scale (1"=1 mile) with 100-foot contour intervals and 1:250,000 scale (1"=3.95 miles) with 200-foot contour intervals. The 1"=1 mile is the one I would recommend. It gives the greatest detail and is, therefore, easier to read.

These maps of Alaska can be ordered by mail from the **U.S. Geological Survey** (U.S.G.S.), Western Distribution Branch, Box 25286, Federal Center, Building 81, Denver, CO 80225. Write for their free Map Index. In Alaska, these can be purchased from the **Alaska Distribution Section**, U.S.G.S., Box 12, Federal Building, Room 126, 101 12th Avenue, Fairbanks, AK 99701.

The maps can be obtained over the counter at the above two locations, or in U.S.G.S. offices in Anchorage, 4230 University Drive (Room 101), or 701 "C" Street (Room F-146) – the large federal building near downtown Anchorage. Many commercial dealers also sell U.S.G.S. maps, but don't depend on those sources at the last minute as their supply may be depleted.

For each trail in this book I have indicated which of the U.S.G.S. maps should be obtained. You can order by the index numbers shown (for example Seward B-1, C-1). If you request these by mail, allow plenty of time.

Plan your trip carefully using a map. Store it in a ZipLock bag to protect it from the weather. Experienced hikers will fold it to show the particular section of the route being covered and put it in a large-size ZipLock bag, allowing visibility in the rain or fog without damaging the map.

➲ Fold the maps into a useful size for carrying in a pouch or pocket. If you wish, cut the border off one map and tape it to the continuing one. You may even trim some unnecessary parts for ease of handling. Don't cut too much; you never know when you may have to make a detour or just want to extend portions of your trip.

CONTACTING AGENCIES

Agencies are typically not set up to answer a lot of calls. The person you need to talk to may be in a conference, in the field, or working on a project. Plus, the answer to your question may take more thought than just a quick response over the telephone. For these reasons, contact is best made via mail. The land managing agency is listed for each of the trails throughout this book.

Here is what I normally do. Write for any printed material, including maps, about the particular area or trail. Ask in the letter if there is a staff person who can answer specific questions and if it is possible to call and speak with that person directly. They may even suggest particular days of the week or hours of the day when someone is available. Be sure to have very specific questions written down in front of you before picking up the phone. This avoids wasted time on both ends.

CHECKING LATEST CONDITIONS

This is where telephone calls to the agencies can pay off. Local trail conditions may be quite different than normally depicted in the literature depending upon current weather patterns. These are often hard to predict when you live 100 miles away or, worse yet, 1,000 miles away.

The agencies monitor local weather conditions as best they can and will share this information with you. Even if they do not have the latest information, their experience certainly makes them better predictors of the effect of a local storm or a changing weather front.

→ Checking local conditions is especially important where weather patterns are unstable and during the winter in mountainous terrain.

CHOOSING THE RIGHT TRAIL

Most trails lead to someplace special – a beautiful mountain lake, a scenic overlook, or a stream chock-full of silver-sided salmon. First, you must decide the kind of landscape best suited to the type of activities you wish to pursue. And keep in mind that the setting often changes depending on the season, the migration of a species like caribou, the weather patterns and even the local climatic conditions that bring on wildflower displays or the ripening of wild berries. The exciting part about Southcentral is that there are so many different choices in landscapes, seasonal changes and types of trails.

Recognition of your personal constraints is another issue. Trips taken with young children limit where you can go, but they often are the most rewarding because you get to share with them your values and ideals about enjoying the great out-of-doors.

Some other important considerations for the more challenging trails are: (1) **The limits of your skills.** There are places I just won't go because I do not have technical climbing skills. You can often get to that certain promontory by just scrambling over rocks and not risking life and limb to get there. (2) **Your level of conditioning**. If you go through an Alaskan winter, you will probably not be in top form when the snow melts, unless you are a die-hard cross-country skier. (3) **Seasonal conditions.** Landscapes that are inviting in the summer may be very inhospitable in the fall and winter. Contact the responsible agency about such conditions before venturing forth.

If all trails lead somewhere, it would be nice to know where they go, what to expect and what conditions you might encounter. The succeeding chapters tell you just that. They give an overview of the regions and the location of the trails. Then each trail is described in terms of the primary attractors, seasonal timing, the environmental setting and any constraints, such as poor travel terrain or hazardous conditions.

CHOOSING THE RIGHT EQUIPMENT

The equipment you need will depend on where you are going, what you plan to do on the trip and how long you will be gone. Without the proper gear, at best, you may not have a very enjoyable experience; at worst, you may find yourself in a life-threatening situation. It is not necessary to buy a whole new outfit because you are now in Alaska; your existing equipment should work fine. You just need to be prepared for the vagaries of weather and natural hazards.

PACKS

Packs need to be large enough to accommodate your gear, including emergency provisions and any additional items you may want to pack out. Plus, they should be comfortable to wear over extended periods of time. Packs come with internal or external frames. I used a large external frame for years, but recently switched to an internal frame with all of its hip and belt padding and an adjustable harness. I now can carry more load and still feel very comfortable. The choice is yours.

If you are looking for a new pack, narrow the choices down based on your needs, then put the finalists to a hiking test. Fill them with weight and volume similar to what you normally carry and go for a hike – even if it is downtown Anchorage. Most sporting goods stores will help you properly adjust the harness and give you the opportunity to try out the packs. The one thing you don't want to do is *not* try out the pack. This is just as important for your daypack as it is for your overnight backpack.

TENTS

A tent is essential even if you are hiking to a public-use cabin. I always carry my three-pound, two-person backpack tent; you never know when you might need it. This has proved to be a lifesaver more than once. Recently, I had to use the tent on the way to a public-use cabin when the wind-driven snow obliterated the trail just before dark. It got cold that night and snowed some more. Ironically, when the weather lifted the next morning, I was only a half-mile from the cabin.

A tent should be lightweight, free-standing, water resistant and durable under strong winds. Plus, it should be easy to assemble and break down. Color may not be of great importance to you, but it is a consideration. Bright reds, blues and yellows stand out on the landscape. I personally try to blend in, particularly if I am above timberline. My brown camouflage material blends in to minimize my visual intrusion on others – including the critters I am trying to observe and photograph.

> ➲   If you want to extend your tent space, take some heavy-duty plastic bags and use them to store some of your gear outside, such as your backpack and cook set.

STOVES AND COOKING EQUIPMENT

In choosing your stove, remember that you have to pack it in and out, so weight is a consideration. It should not only be compact and lightweight, but also should put out a hot flame and burn efficiently. Sounds like a tall order? Not really. There are a number of stoves that will do the job. I prefer the gasoline types to propane or butane. Under normal use, one bottle of white gas will last me about three to four days. However, these types of stoves do carbon up and must be periodically cleaned. Take an extra cleaning wire on your trip.

> ➲   Cleaning wires can get broken easily. Keep an extra one taped to a piece of cardboard in your map pocket.

Cooksets can be as elaborate as you want. Some prefer a multi-pan set for cooking different food. These can be aluminum or stainless steel. I prefer an aluminum deep pot with a lid because it is lightweight and will boil enough water at one time for a complete meal of freeze-dried food for two people, with some leftover for a hot drink. The lid is essential for efficiently boiling water.

For transporting, I store my stove, minus the gas bottle, in a clean ZipLock bag in the aluminum pot. A large rubber band then keeps the lid in place. In backpacking, not only is weight important, but also volume. I jump at any opportunity to reduce either or both without sacrificing comfort and efficiency.

SLEEPING BAGS/MATTRESS

A good sleeping bag and mattress are essential to an enjoyable overnight hike. The weight of the sleeping bag must be matched to the expected temperatures. I have several bags I can choose from, but most people stick with a single bag. In that case, it should be sufficient to cope with the worst conditions you normally encounter. Or you can choose a bag to meet normal conditions and add a liner to increase warmth during the colder seasons. You can always unzip the bag in warmer weather – even sleep on top if it is really hot.

I prefer Fiber Fill rather than goose down because of the wet weather. Quallofil is my first choice because it compacts well into the stuff sack, maintains its loft and remains warm, even when wet. There are also many new fibers on the market, such as Lite-loft, which should be more than acceptable. Given the opportunity, you should always air your sleeping bag to get rid of the moisture given off by your body and to make it smell fresher.

Do not expect to sleep on smooth, flat cushy ground. It never works out that way. It is easy enough to laugh about it now, but I always seem to end up camping on rough ground, sloping in the wrong direction. You are never going to find the perfect place to sleep in the outdoors. Thus, it is important to have a good mattress pad to "smooth out" the site and keep you insulated from the cold soil. Closed-cell foam pads don't seem to do either very well, but are somewhat compact. The open cell does better but doesn't compact very well. I prefer the Thermarest mattress because it meets both requirements of smoothing the site and keeping you warm, plus it compacts for easy storage. There are similar mattresses now on the market. If the trip is short with minimal other equipment, I take my 72" regular mattress. For the longer trips with heavier packs, I take the ultralight one, which compacts into a small drawstring bag.

CAMP EQUIPMENT

Other camp equipment you should consider:
- **Folding saw**. Depending on your needs, a saw may be very desirable in camp for anything from cutting firewood to opening a moose rib cage. I prefer a three- or four-sided collapsible bow saw; it is rigid and enables me to make long, smooth strokes without busting my knuckles.

- **Knife**. My favorite is the multi-element Swiss Army knife.
- **Water container.** It is important to take water with you or be able to retrieve it some distance from your campsite, particularly in the mountain alpine areas in the middle of the summer.
- **Compass.** An essential piece of equipment. Learn to use it.
- **Waterproof match container**, matches and fire starter.
- **Large, heavy duty plastic bag**s. Use them to sort and protect items in your pack and around camp.

CAMERA/BINOCULARS

Always take your camera and binoculars. If it is not specifically a photographic trip, take a small camera with fixed focus. Pack adequate film stored in a ZipLock bag. Binoculars are a must, too. Leave them home and you will regret it. You may never get to see the beautiful colors of a migrating duck or the stark contrast where two rock strata come together halfway up a nearby ridge. Some people prefer the small, fixed-focus camera and ultralight binoculars. While I have tried these, I like the luxury of my SLR camera with telephoto lens and full-size binoculars. This is one area where I do not skimp on weight and volume. You may never return to some places.

WEAPONS

When you go on a hunt, you obviously take a weapon. But what about other times? When you go into bear country, you should consider some sort of bear protection. I prefer an ultralight .308 rifle because it easily straps to the side of the pack. I do not recommend pistols. Short-barreled shotguns with slugs and buckshot are acceptable. Whatever you choose, get adequate instruction and spend sufficient time at the rifle range to learn how to shoot. Then spend some time with a person who has experienced bears up close. You need to know not only *how* to use the weapon, but also *when*. See *Wildlife* in the next chapter.

One such weapon per hiking group should be sufficient if you stay close to one another. I definitely do not favor having lots of weapons in camp. Weapons are not allowed in certain portions of Alaska's National Parks. If in doubt, contact the particular park.

EMERGENCY PROVISIONS

Emergency provisions are important whether you are on a day hike or a week-long trip. These items should include:

	Weight (oz.)
1. Emergency survival blanket	3
2. Emergency mylar sleeping bag	4
3. Tube tent, one- or two-man	5-9
4. Pocket first aid kit	8
5. Acrylic signal mirror	1
6. Waterproof matches, container and fire starter	3
7. Aerial flares	6
8. Small stuff sack	2
Total weight	32 - 36 oz. (2 -2¼ lbs.)

I have recently been able to purchase all of these directly from **School of Survival Specialties** (P.O. Box 7225, Spokane, WA). You do not use these items very often and you may be tempted to leave them home to make room for something else, despite the fact that they take up very little space. Don't.

➲ Keep an eye on the expiration dates for all of your emergency equipment. A group of us tested our kits over a weekend last year. Some things worked and others, because of age, did not. Practice using and replacing them periodically.

Remember that your life and those of others may depend on these provisions. I even take CPR and first aid refresher courses when available just to be prepared for some emergency that I hope never occurs.

There are a few other things you might want to add to your emergency provisions: moleskin, aspirin, ointment for rashes or cuts and any special medicine you may personally require.

The signal mirror works well with some sunlight. Practice with the mirror because it can be difficult to use. It is effective, as tested on several airplanes during a recent survival training. The flares are more effective during low light or darkness.

CHOOSING THE RIGHT FOOD

It goes without saying that hikers should take high-energy, lightweight foods that are simple to prepare. The obvious choices are freeze-dried food from the specialty stores and instant dehydrated foods from the grocery. I choose much of my backpack food from the grocer's shelf. All of these foods have been improved since they were first introduced and are generally very tasty. Beverages are also a consideration – from tea bags and instant coffee to Tang, hot or cold. It is important that you keep a lot of liquids in you and available; they add quick energy.

Rather than try to go through all the various foods, I will simply share my menus of a typical day on the trail. For breakfast, I like something quick, but hot. Instant oats, in all flavors, are a favorite of mine. If it is going to be a tough day on the trail, I will eat two packets mixed with hot water right in my drinking cup. A few drops of hot water are then used to rinse the cup for my hot coffee, tea or Tang. Half an English muffin with a squeeze of marmalade is eaten with the tea. These muffins are a good choice because they taste good, do not crumble or compact and do not get stale. I finish off breakfast with a granola bar and more hot drink. On hot summer mornings, I may substitute granola cereal for oatmeal.

For mid-morning and mid-afternoon snacks, I prefer homemade jerky (from a moose or caribou roast) and half an English muffin with a little cheese from the squeeze tube off the grocer's shelf (it never needs refrigeration!). I then top this with a drink of water and a handful or two of trail mix – nuts, M&M's, raisins and small pieces of dried fruit.

For lunch, I may repeat my mid-morning snack if the going is not too difficult. If it is cold, I will take time to heat up water for instant soup and tea. The intent is to take in plenty of energy and liquids, but not eat too much at one time, which can lead to feeling sluggish.

I always look forward to supper. Maybe it is relaxing around camp in the evening with good friends that gives it a warm feeling. This is where I use freeze-dried meals. You can get any of your favorite main dishes in freeze-dried form. They taste good, too. It usually takes about 5-10 minutes for the hot water to completely rehydrate everything in the pack. While waiting, I will have a cup of hot chocolate, then some tea after the meal. It is important to drink plenty of liquids during and after supper so you do not get cramps in the night. If it has been a good day on the trail – and even if it wasn't such a good day – I may indulge in something really decadent like a piece of chocolate.

While freeze-dried foods are important to your backpacking diet, you can find lightweight good quality food right on your grocer's shelf. Take some home and try it before you head out on a hiking adventure. Find the things that are high energy. Make sure you like what you choose. Believe me, it's important that you look forward to that mid-morning snack or evening meal.

Always take more food than you need because you could be out an extra day or two for unforeseen reasons. If you are going to be in a general area or returning over the same route, you could cache your extra food in a sturdy waterproof bag. Ideally, you would want to suspend it between two trees out of reach of critters. Above timberline, you might dig a safe place under a stream bank and then line it with a plastic bag. Only do this if the weight is such that you don't want to carry the extra food for the whole trip. Remember, a cache is not foolproof and there is a chance that it may not be there when you return.

CHOOSING THE RIGHT CLOTHING

In Alaska, you have to prepare for the worst because the weather can change so fast. I have seen it go from warm and sunny to cloudy and misty, then rain and snow – all within an hour. Summer days and even some fall days can be very warm. But they can also be very wet and cool, if not cold. Without the right clothing, you could find yourself in a very miserable, if not dangerous, situation.

Because you need to prepare for the vagaries of the weather and still keep bulk and weight down in your pack, layering clothing is essential. With modern fabrics and good lightweight clothing design, it is possible to take the minimal clothing, weightwise, and still be prepared.

The first layer is the **underwear**. I prefer synthetics like Cool Max and take extra briefs. Polypropylene long johns may be packed in your backpack or worn as necessary. Polypropylene does not absorb moisture. In fact, it wicks moisture away from your skin. Some people prefer the newer polyester, but I still stick with my "polypros."

The next layer is your **normal outer garment**. I like my Polartec pants for summer and heavier wools for winter. Wool still insulates even if it gets wet. I normally wear a medium- to heavyweight Polartec or Worsterlon shirt, depending on expected temperatures. A Polartec 300 jacket or wool sweater is worn over the top of this. If temperatures become very cold, a heavy jacket may be substituted.

The last layer is the **outer garment**, which should be waterproof and can also be insulating. Gortex pants and coat, or other modern lightweight fabrics, are ideal. To this an insulation could be bonded. Remember your raingear can also protect you from the chilling effects of the wind. I am not a fan of the poncho or the expanded poncho (over the pack) because it blows so much in the wind. I take a cover to protect the backpack against the rain. I do have a three-quarter-length rain jacket that I wear with my hipboots, without rainpants. This makes a good combination for wet weather conditions on shorter hiking trips. In all cases, I take a baseball hat to wear under the hood of the rain jacket. It helps to push the hood away from my eyes when I turn my head. Try it.

All else equal, the difference between staying warm or not is how well you take care of the extremities – head, hands and feet. In the summer I wear a baseball cap and take a silk or polypropylene balaclava in my shirt pocket. The combination keeps my head warm and works well under my raincoat hood. In fall I add my wool knit hat.

Never go anywhere without a **pair of gloves**. I prefer wool or polypropylene/wool. For really cold weather, you should switch to mittens. Pile mittens with a Gortex outer shell make a good combination.

The best **boots** are the ones that are light enough construction-wise to do the job and fit your feet. Remember that every pound on your feet is like carrying five additional pounds on your back. They must be well broken-in before you wear them on a long hike. Some people wear tennis shoes, but I personally don't think they give enough support. For me, the best hiking boot is the ankle-fit, vibram-soled one – light- to heavyweight construction, depending on your needs. A sewn-in Gortex liner is a nice addition. A smooth leather outer surface allows for easy cleaning and waterproofing. Cleaning and waterproofing is essential; not only will it keep your feet dry, but it will make the boot last.

Your **socks** are essential in keeping your feet dry and comfortable. I usually go with the layering here, using a pair of nylon or polypropylene liner socks and a pair of wool or woolblend outer socks. The polypropylene wicks the moisture away from your feet, the wool insulates and the two layers combined allow movement with minimum friction on your heels. With fresh socks to trade-off along the trip, your feet should stay dry, comfortable and blister-free. All extra clothes should be stored in a plastic bag to keep them dry and in one location in your pack. Moleskin or other foot padding should be a part of your gear. The minute you feel anything wrong with your feet, stop and take care of them.

Please note, there is no "standard" clothing and equipment list. Everyone that I have ever read about or talked to seems to have his or her own. Whatever works best for you is what you should go with. Remember to add your personal toiletry which, as always, should be kept to a minimum. Experiment with new equipment. My only caution is not to try a number of items on a single long-distance hiking trip. They may fail you when you need them most.

GETTING YOUR SUPPLIES THERE

It is awfully tempting to have someone take your supplies and equipment in by boat, horse or airplane. Or, you may have them air-dropped later. Don't. Never, ever separate people from their supplies and equipment. You may get into a whiteout or get lost and need them immediately.

A view of the mountains, summer snowfields and glaciers.

THE MENTAL PREPARATION

THINKING AHEAD

Alaska has a mystique that attracts people to its wild and undeveloped landscape. Even those of us who have lived here for awhile find it as attractive as the day we arrived. This raw, natural quality may, at times, seem fickle. You may find yourself pitted against the very elements that attracted you – the steep talus slopes of the alpine zone made slick by the rainshower, the roaring torrent of a stream that early this morning was placid, a tent torn to shreds by a black bear – probably the one you were filming down by the stream that morning – or you simply got lost. There are probably worse scenarios one could imagine. It is crucial that you consider all scenarios and develop appropriate strategies to deal with them ahead of time.

ESTABLISHING A ROUTE AND ITINERARY

Probably 99% of the time nothing eventful will happen on a hiking trip, but you have to be prepared. One of the first decisions is to establish a route. If you are going to hike 15 miles between trailhead A and trailhead B, that becomes your route. If you plan to camp halfway in between and explore the side drainage to the west, then this becomes part of your route. Plus, when you get to trailhead B, you may plan to climb down to the river to fish. This also becomes part of your route.

Wherever you plan to travel becomes your expected route. You should get a contour map (see above) and lay out your expected route. Put an itinerary with it. Show where you will likely camp so that one can determine approximately where you will be and when. This will help you to assess your progress along your route. Plus, it will help others to locate you in case of an emergency. Certainly no one would expect you to identify your exact location for each part of every day on the trail, but the more detail you can offer before you go, the better.

Within reason, you should stick close to your original route and itinerary.

NOTIFYING A FRIEND

Once that route and itinerary has been established on the map, leave a copy with a friend. It could pay dividends. Once when I was sheep hunting, a family emergency required that the air taxi service locate me as soon as possible. I had told him what side drainage we would be in. He found us with minimum air time, dropped a note wrapped around a rock and picked us up the next morning – where he had originally dropped us off.

Recently, a hiker was rescued because he stuck to his general plan and notified a friend of his route and expected time of return. His intended route was easily identifiable on a large-scale map and from the air. The troopers were notified of his late return and initial reconnaissance flights along the expected route buzzed every cabin en route in search of the missing person. The hiker emerged from one of the cabins and waved. A helicopter later rescued him. The hiker had lost his pack and gear while crossing a river and sought refuge in the cabin. There was a good ending because a route and itinerary were established and a friend notified authorities when the person did not show up. Remember it is your responsibility to have someone to check on your return and notify authorities if necessary. Agencies are not set up to keep track of your route/itinerary.

CHECK WEATHER PATTERNS

In Southeast Alaska they say, "Don't plan on a boating trip. Just get ready and, if the weather cooperates, go." The same could be said for other areas where the weather patterns are influenced by the maritime climate, or high altitude. Rain is no reason to stay home. You could end up at your house most of the time! It is the storm fronts that are of concern. These are predictable; and a call to your local weather station prior to departure will stand you in good stead. However, you should also consider calling the responsible agency to see if they can translate that forecast into impacts on local conditions. For example, a storm front may produce intermittent rain at lower elevations, but the cooling effect at higher elevations, particularly in the narrow sheltered valleys through which your travel route passes, may produce a heavy fog – almost whiteout conditions. While these conditions may not be life-threatening, if you know in advance their likely effects, you may decide to shift your hike from the west side of the peninsula to the east. Even if you do not shift, you can now go better prepared for whatever weather you might encounter.

KNOW YOUR BOUNDARIES

It is important that you know how to read your topographic map and orient yourself to the land features around you. Some may say that is not important if you are on a trail; you cannot get lost. But it is important because you want to know where you are along the trail, or you may reach a point where the trail becomes indistinct before dropping down into a canyon. You need to keep your bearings.

➲ For those traveling with children, using the interesting names of the surrounding peaks and rivers can be a fun way to get them used to keeping track of their location.

One way to keep yourself from getting lost – either because the trail becomes unclear, you took a side trip or you missed the turnoff onto a secondary trail – is to set boundaries along your route. Do what pilots do: The pilot who is going to fly up to Valley Hot Springs will set his boundaries at Toad River to the north, Belle Creek in the east and the Crazy Mountains to the west. Because the hot springs and the small landing strip are not easy to locate from a distance, the pilot uses these easily identifiable boundaries to frame his target. Without such boundaries, the pilot may simply fly straight ahead looking for the hot springs – and really get lost.

By being aware of these boundaries, you should recognize when you are getting close to your destination or when you have gone too far and need to turn back. If you have chosen good boundaries, make them inviolate. Once you bump up against them, make an appropriate turn to find your nearby destination point. Do not begin second guessing yourself.

PRACTICING SAFETY

- **Know your limits**. Do not push beyond your limits. You can become exhausted, disoriented, or place yourself in a precarious position that you do not have the strength, stamina or skills to fully deal with.
- **Know first aid**. Develop your skills in first aid and CPR. Hopefully none of us will ever have to treat anything worse than a cut or blister, but you never know. I try to refresh my skills through community-sponsored evening courses. It is amazing the changes in first aid techniques that have occurred over time. Plus, those courses give you supervised practice that we all need.
- **Take proper equipment, food and clothing**. You must be prepared.
- **Take your emergency gear** – regardless of the length of the trip.
- **Bearproof yourself**. Purchase bear repellent made of red pepper or take a firearm. Know how and when to use both.
- **Stick to your route/itinerary**. If someone needs to contact you, or a search party starts to look for your missing hiking group, they can only look within your known route. This assumes that you filed your hiking plan with a friend.
- **Remain flexible in your decision-making**. While it is important to stick to your intended route and itinerary, some things may dictate that you alter your route – an irate bear that chased another hiking group farther up on the trail, or a small stream that you can normally wade but is now high and swift because of upstream snow melt. Never feel you must absolutely reach your destination right on time. Spend the night near the stream and cross early in the morning when the stream should be at its lowest level (the cool night having reduced snow melt), or return to your original starting point without reaching your destination. Do not take unnecessary chances. Think through your options and make the best choice under the

circumstances. Notify your friend or authorities as soon as you can, if you are overdue.

SPECIAL ALASKAN HAZARDS

HYPOTHERMIA

This is the lowering of internal body temperature, which leads to mental lapses, disorientation and ultimately physical collapse. It is caused by exposure to cold, wetness (from rain, a fall while crossing a stream or simply your own perspiration), wind chill on your wet clothes and physical exhaustion. Ironically, hypothermia typically does not occur at very low temperatures as we are normally prepared for those conditions. Most cases occur between 30°F and 50°F.

The **U.S. Forest Service Winter Recreation Safety Guide** recommends appointing a foul-weather "leader" to check for obvious symptoms of hypothermia. Because of the mental lapses, the victim often refuses to admit that there is anything wrong. Symptoms are shivering, sometimes uncontrollably, slow or slurred speech, memory lapses, fumbling hands, stumbling and then incoherence.

Prevention is best. Wear polypropylene long johns, Polartec or wool clothing, good rain gear and proper boots. Avoid exhausting yourself. Mild cases may be treated by exercising, drinking warm liquids and eating high-caloric foods.

Treatment for more severe cases involves eliminating the causes – set up your tent or whatever makeshift shelter is available to get out of the cold, rain and wind. Concentrate on making the camp comfortable. Remove wet clothes and replace them with dry ones. Put the person into the best insulated bag on hand. Keep them awake and slowly feed warm liquids. In the worst cases an external source of heat is necessary. Putting the stripped victim into a sleeping bag with another near-naked person allows for skin-to-skin contact, giving the most efficient transfer of body heat. In fact, if you can zip two bags together, put the victim between two warm bodies.

In the worst scenario – and taking into consideration the current weather conditions – you should send another team member to request a medical evacuation while initiating treatment of the victim. Remember that the body temperature can be lowered so much that a heart beat may not be detectable. Apply the treatment and continue to check for a heartbeat. Never immediately assume that death has occurred.

GLACIERS AND GLACIAL STREAMS

The novice should stay away from glaciers unless guided by an experienced glacial climber with the proper equipment. There are two potential problems with this beautiful environment: falling into a crevasse and having large blocks of ice fall on you around the toe of the glacier.

Crevasses are often difficult to see because they are covered with a new snow crust. A lady recently fell into a crevasse on Byron Glacier in the middle of the winter. She was less than a mile from her car and had traveled a designated trail, but several people were actually on Byron Glacier at the time, so she was tempted to join them. Fortunately, there was someone on the scene who was familiar with glacier rescue. He put his own life in danger by crawling head-first into the crevasse to get a rope around her. Yes, it was a happy ending, but the next time it may not be. Do not be afraid of glaciers, but enjoy them from the proper distance.

Glacial streams are created by melting glaciers. They are cold, silt laden, and can be very deep and swift. I have stood by a glacial river in August and listened to large boulders being rolled by the force of the water until they break apart . I have also waded across that same spot at the end of September when the water was less than knee deep and clear enough to see the bottom.

I do not recommend crossing large glacial streams at any time. They are just too dangerous. For the smaller streams, look for the wider, shallower crossings. I often take along an old pair of tennis shoes for crossing creeks. Another trick, if your boots are well greased, is to put on your rain pants and pull them down over the tops of your boots. Place a rubber band or tie around the bottom of each leg so that it is snug around the top of each boot. This works okay if you have only one or two crossings.

At your chosen crossing, face upstream at a 45° angle. Always move in that 45° angle direction. The force of the water will typically bring your actual course nearly straight across to the other side. Undo the buckle on your waist strap so it is easy to get your pack off if you fall. You can use a walking stick for support. Take short steps and feel the bottom. You do not want to stand on loose rocks and lose your balance. You may need to help shorter, lighter people by having them follow you on the downstream side. If necessary, drop your pack and carry others across on your back. (They must hang on tightly without moving so your arms are free for balancing.) You can also use a rope and walk people across one at a time. Never tie a rope around anyone. They may fall, get tangled in the rope and drown.

If you do fall and are swept downstream, drop your pack, roll onto your back and face downstream with your feet in front of you. Lay back and bring your feet up to push off objects. Turn 45° and do a backstroke to pull yourself toward shore. Once on shore, assume the worst and treat for hypothermia.

> ➲ Remember, glacial streams are at their lowest early in the summer and early in the morning. Watch the weather and be prepared to take an alternate route if necessary. A prolonged rain spell followed by warm sunny days could make any creek impassable.

WILDLIFE

Most wildlife can be unpredictable, but there are two critters you must be particularly aware of: **cow moose with calves** and **bears**, black or grizzly. Cow moose are particularly sensitive to any perceived danger to their calves. If you surprise one on the trail she will run from you, given an escape route. But if you find yourself between her and her calf, you've got trouble on your hands. In Alaska, probably more people have been attacked by moose than bear. This is particularly true in early summer. Retreat if you can. Do it as quickly as you can without running. Keep your eye on the cow. If there is a tree to climb, drop your pack and climb it. The cow will rear and flail with its front feet when charging. One blow could leave you severely wounded. If you are up a tree, stay there until you are certain that the cow moose has left. Mother moose can be persistent.

Now, let's talk about bears. Bears are to be respected, but if you do your part you shouldn't have any problems. Bears encountered on a trail, unless you surprise them at close range, will most likely head for the next drainage. You can warn bears by loud talking or by wearing a bell clipped to your pack. The bear will leave before you get too close.

Bears around camp tend to be more of a problem. They are curious animals and are attracted by the smells of a free lunch. Keep your camp clean. Cook and store your food a safe distance from your tent. In bear country I prefer to use freeze-dried food and burn the container after eating. Anything left over after that, I store in a plastic bag away from camp and pack out at the end of the trip. This keeps smells away from camp.

In forested country, I set up my camp well away from the trail and cache my food in a heavy plastic bag secured by a rope high in a tree. In alpine country, where you have to cache your food on the ground, I place it in a white plastic bag at least 100 yards away directly in front of the tent so it is easy to see when I open the flap. If the white bag is gone, I become fully alert almost immediately. Also, I run a loosely tied cord through the stove, pot and lid so that any movement of these items in the night makes lots of noise.

Black bears may seem cuddly, but they can be dangerous. Though I have never had trouble from them, I have had several bears in my camp nosing around curiously. They are on their worst behavior when hungry and when protecting cubs. As with moose, if you get between a mother and her young, you are in for trouble. Back out gracefully, climb a tree, etc. – whatever is your best escape route. Often a bear will move closer, stand on its hind legs and snort just to figure out what you are. If a bear is aware of your presence, but is still some distance away, you should make a lot of noise, stand tall and act mean. It will look strange to other humans, but might serve to intimidate a bear.

Treat the grizzlies the same as you would black bears. It has been my experience that the younger, 2½- to 3-year-old bears have the worst manners. They have not learned to be afraid of man.

As already stated, I do carry a weapon – a 5½-pound ultralight .308 rifle with 180-grain cartridges in the magazine, not in the chamber. It straps conveniently to the side of my pack, and that is where it stays unless we pass through thick brush in bear country. It remains right beside me in the tent at night. Have I ever shot a bear in self-protection? No. And they have come as close as 50 feet. Any closer and I would have fired a warning shot. I never have. Maybe it is because I smell bad on the trail or spew out all those unmentionable words when I am yelling at them.

The final consideration is what to do if you are charged by a bear!

- ◆ Remain standing, make yourself appear as big and tall as you can and shout at the bear.
- ◆ **Do not run.** You cannot outrun a bear. He then sees you as weak prey and will attack.
- ◆ If you are knocked down or grabbed by the bear, play dead. Assume the fetal position, lying primarily on your stomach and clasp your hands behind your neck to protect the

vertebrae. Remain quiet and motionless. If the bear thinks you are "dead," it may simply drop you and leave the area. It may scratch leaves and twigs over you to create a food cache. Try to remain conscious, but do not move. Let the bear leave, then quickly depart in the opposite direction.

DRINKING WATER

You would think that the water found in the wilds of Alaska would be the cleanest, purist of anywhere in the United States. It certainly looks that way. But the microorganism *Giardia lamblia* occurs in a cystic form in Alaskan lakes and streams. The disease it causes is called **giardiasis** or **beaver fever**. After ingestion, it attaches to the small intestine causing diarrhea, abdominal cramps and bloating. Loss of appetite and general nausea are also symptoms. It is not typically life-threatening, but you could not convince the victim of this while on a long backpack trip.

The symptoms may not be apparant for a few days. In fact, you may have already returned home before they show. Unfortunately they may last for several weeks. Advise your physician about the possibility of *giardiasis*, even if you are not sure. Without treatment, the symptoms may persist intermittently over an even longer period of time. The disease is curable with prescribed medication.

To avoid contracting beaver feaver, treat your drinking water. Boil water for five minutes, or treat it with iodine tablets; some outdoorsfolk recommend doing both. Some portable water filters will work, if they filter out particles as small as one micron. Read the specifications in the literature. I also drink directly from the stream when I am well above timberline and have never had a problem, but I do not encourage it.

This brings me to another concern about drinking water – lack of it in the alpine zone. There are many places where water is nonexistent by mid- to late summer. If you are traveling into new country in the alpine zone, carry water with you, pick it up at the last point where water is readily available, or be willing to drop off the ridge considerable distances to get water when you make camp in the evening. This book does not indicate if water sources are found along particular trails above timberline. It can vary throughout the summer and from summer to summer. My advice is always to assume that it is scarce.

WHITEOUTS

Whiteouts, where a combination of snow and fog obliterate the landscape, make travel very difficult and even hazardous. This can occur at any season in the high country, particularly above timberline. If you can see it coming, retreat below timberline and wait it out. If you are caught above timberline, make yourself comfortable and, again, wait for it to pass. It is dangerous to wander around in a whiteout; you could fall from a cliff or simply get lost. Remember this is a prime time for hypothermia to set in. You are wet with sweat, the temperature suddenly drops 20°F and you are stuck in one location. If nothing else, you should have your emergency gear. Pull out the emergency blanket and tube tent and crawl inside to enjoy some trail mix. Or, you could fix a hot drink if you have your stove along. If nothing else is available to keep warm, you could light a square of firestarter, drape the emergency blanket around you and squat over the fire. The main reason for retreating below timberline is because the vegetation breaks up the intensity of the whiteout and the well-defined trail gives one the option of returning to the trailhead. There is also a better chance of finding wood for a fire there.

STEEP, ROCKY TERRAIN

For the most part the trails presented in this book are not located in steep, hazardous terrain. Certainly cross-country routes and side trips are often done in the alpine zones, where there is the potential to find oneself in hazardous places. It is usually easy enough to see what you might be getting into and avoid hazards. I advise that you always return to the trail via the same route you used to get there. Be aware that you can get into trouble quickly coming down a precipitous slope if you slide down to a point where you cannot go further down or retreat back up the slope. Also, remember that it is easier to climb *up* a precipitous slope than to climb down. The problems of maneuvering on steep slopes are made even worse by rain or a light amount of wet snow.

AVALANCHES

Many people will be using the same trails in the winter. Where there are known avalanche problems, these are mentioned in the description of individual trails. Any avalanche can be life-threatening and the only safe technique is to avoid them. If there is any concern, call the responsible managing agency about local conditions. If you are a winter "buff" and normally travel in hazardous areas, it is imperative you read about and/or take a short course in avalanche detection and survival.

COMMON COURTESY ON THE TRAIL

You should be courteous to other hikers and wildlife (whose home you have invaded). Most people are out there for the same purpose as you – to get away from it all. Respect that ideal. When you meet people on the trail, having lunch or setting up camp, give them a friendly hello and keep on hiking, unless they invite you to join them. When you stop to take pictures or eat lunch, move off the trail. I wear earth-toned clothing to keep visual impact to a minimum for others on the trail.

This is doubly important in dealing with wildlife. Summer is the time for building nests and raising young. Any of your activities, particularly the louder, more disruptive ones, can have a drastic impact on individual creatures or family groups. The best advice is to know the habitats and normal behaviors of the most common species and avoid any personal activities that would disturb them. Secondly, be very observant of the wildlife around you so as to avoid startling them or otherwise creating stress.

Photographing wild animals can often be disruptive. Do it from a distance. Use your long lens. Quietly back away after taking your shot. If you cannot work without stressing the animal, then you should not be there. There will be other opportunities.

TRAIL CONDITIONS

Trail conditions can affect your ability to maneuver along a particular trail segment. The general conditions for each trail profiled in this book are discussed in each trail description. Look at these carefully. If conditions are too difficult for your physical or mental condition, you may need to opt for another trail. Don't push yourself beyond your limits.

And conditions change – usually for the worse because of bad weather, floods, or similar problems. Please check with the local managing agency about trail conditions before you attempt a particular trail, particularly if the trip is planned for several days.

MINIMUM IMPACT CAMPING

This "take only photographs and leave only footprints" policy is a good one to follow. Here are some reminders that reinforce this concept:

- ◆ Choose a well-drained site for camping. Do not trench around the tent.
- ◆ Camp away from the trail and any sensitive environment, such as an alpine lake, by at least 200 feet.
- ◆ Burn only dead and down wood. Do not hack on live trees. Keep fires small. Use a lightweight stove.
- ◆ Pack out all trash. Do not bury it.
- ◆ Bury all human waste at least 200 feet from any water source and burn your toilet paper.
- ◆ Do not tie livestock to live trees.
- ◆ Avoid known wildlife concentrations to minimize disruptions of their habitat. Minimize your noise.
- ◆ Use earthtone colors in your choice of tents, gear and clothing.
- ◆ Respect the privacy of other campers.

THE BASICS

This section focuses on the abundant trails and public-use cabins. For those unfamiliar with these cabins, they are provided by a public management agency, usually on a reservation basis, for a fee.

The description of individual trails should help you plan the wheres and whens of your hiking adventures, but it is still essential to contact the managing agencies for up-to-date conditions.

GEOGRAPHY

This section is divided into units or subregions of Southcentral Alaska. Each of these units has a unique physiography. The one thing they have in common is that they all have road access. This doesn't mean that they are intensively roaded. On the contrary, there may be 20 to 40 miles between roads – or there may not be any road at all. Thus, typically you will not encounter many groups on the trail.

The primary port of entry to the region for the nonlocal is via Anchorage International Airport. Anchorage acts as the hub of the road system, with routes radiating down to the Kenai Peninsula and east to the Mat-Su Valley (Palmer-Wasilla area). Get an Alaskan roadmap after arriving here.

There are few roads in Alaska, so it's almost impossible to get lost in a vehicle. If you are not sure, stop and ask. Alaskans are friendly. National car rental companies are readily available at the airport. I recommend that you make reservations well in advance. Public transportation (buses) runs to all of the cities and towns in the Kenai Peninsula and Mat-Su Valley. However, you must still get to the trailheads, which would require a local car rental or shuttle. All cities and towns have local car rental companies. Shuttle services do exist, but are not well known and may not operate from year to year. Ask in the local town if someone is willing to drive you to the trailhead for a fee. If you need to shuttle your car from one trailhead to another, get a local person who will drop your car at the takeout point then take you to your starting point. That way you know your vehicle will be waiting for you.

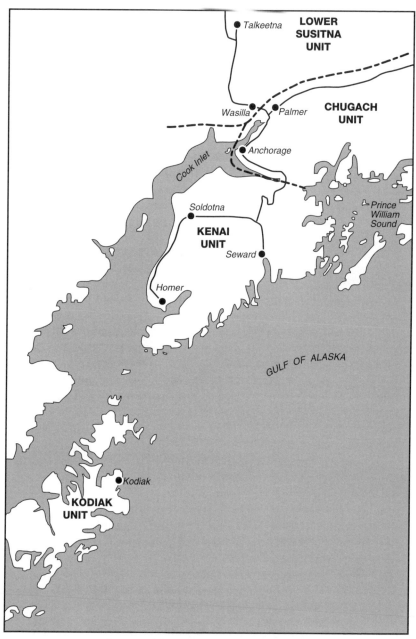

Southcentral Alaska Regional Map
Showing the Four Hiking Units

Southcentral Alaska has been divided into four separate units for presenting the trail descriptions – Kenai, Chugach, Lower Susitna and Kodiak.

SERVICES

Hikers typically need minimal services – trail food, items that were forgotten, last minute information from the agencies, warm showers afterwards and possibly shuttle service. Normal and dehydrated foods are available in any supermarket in the larger towns in Southcentral. Specialized foods and equipment are more available in the Anchorage area at large sporting goods stores and specialty shops. All towns in the Southcentral region have laundromats, and these usually have showers with towel, wash cloth and soap for a nominal fee.

The name and phone number for the managing agency are listed with each trail shown in this section. Use these contacts. They are the best source of up-to-date information.

Most of the national motel chains are represented in the Anchorage area. Reservations can be made through the appropriate 800 numbers, all listed in your *Yellow Pages*. Reservations are essential in the middle of the summer in Anchorage, and motel/hotels can be relatively pricey here. Things tend to be more flexible in the smaller towns, where options are usually better geared to the backpacker's schedule and pocketbook. If there are no vacancies at your first hotel choice, ask for other places you might try. Clerks are willing to make recommendations and might even call them for you.

I have always been very pleased with the service offered at the following motels (all are area code 907):

Wasilla
Lake Lucille Inn 373-1776
Seward
Marina Motel 224-5518
Breeze Inn 224-5238
Cooper Landing
Troutfitters Alpine Motel 595-1212
Kenai/Soldotna
King Salmon Best Western 262-5857

Kings Inn 283-6060
Soldotna Inn. 262-9169
Homer
Beluga Lake Lodge. 235-5995
Bidarka Inn Best Western. 235-8148
Ocean Shores Motel 235-7775

The final recommendation, if you enjoy informality, is to try a Bed and Breakfast. These are scattered all over the region and usually don't require reservations. Plus, they are less expensive and offer excellent opportunities to learn about Alaskana. A guide to B & B's, *Bed and Breakfast Alaska Style,* is published by Kachemak Publishing, P.O. Box 470, Homer, AK 99603.

KENAI UNIT

The Kenai Unit covers the entire Kenai Peninsula from Kachemak Bay to Portage Glacier. The scenery is spectacular. The eastern coastline is dotted with saltwater glaciers that calve into the bays. These glaciers are appendages of two major icefields – Sargent Icefield, north of Seward in the Chugach National Forest, and Harding Icefield, the backbone of Kenai Fjords National Park south of Seward. Also part of this eastern zone is the alpine country of the Kenai Mountains – the beautiful landscapes bathed in summer wildflowers, dotted with alpine lakes and home of the Dall sheep, mountain goat and black bear. This region is rich in early native culture and mining. Many historic coastal exploration routes are now recreational trails.

HISTORY

You, too, can follow the footsteps of the early explorers and miners over such routes as the Resurrection Pass Trail and the Iditarod Trail, as well as to lesser known places. Our forefathers pushed inland to explore the lands and resources and to test their skills against the rawness of nature. They found a scenically rich environment full of "exotic" plants and animals, returning to their homelands with many stories to tell. We can do the same things – explore the wilds, test our outdoor skills and share our experiences with others. The only difference is style – we call it recreation.

THE LAND

The western half of the Peninsula is primarily bottomland covered with spruce, boggy in places, but home to many rivers and lakes. The largest river – the Kenai – is really a system of rivers that feeds the Kenai River main stem. While there are fishable lakes scattered over the eastern part of the Peninsula, the three largest – Kenai, Skilak and Tustemena – offer limited fishing because they are primarily fed by glacial streams.

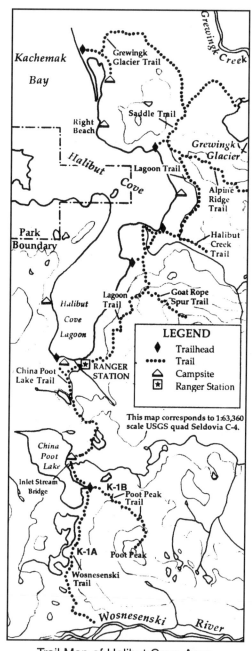

Trail Map of Halibut Cove Area

WILDLIFE

What is this zone famous for? Salmon and moose. The world's largest king salmon come from the Kenai River, and all major streams offer some species of salmon to fish. Check the fishing regulations before planning a trip. Some streams or portions are closed to protect spawning populations.

The gigantic Alaskan moose can be seen along the waterways in this region of Southcentral. They seem so big that you wonder how they get through the bottomland brush. Yet, they do it... and very gracefully.

FYI

While each of us is directed by something inside us, it usually takes a spark from a pilot light to turn us on. To me, the Kenai offers many pilot lights. All we have to do is expose ourselves.

The trails for The Kenai Unit are numbered alpha numerically (e.g. K-2) and shown on corresponding maps.

Looking across Kachemak Bay to Kachemak Bay State Park.

TRAILS

KACHEMAK BAY STATE PARK TRAIL SYSTEM (K-1)

Unique Attractions:	Easy family hiking in low country. Access to alpine zone for viewing scenery and wildlife.
Area Description:	Most of the trail segments are in the lowland spruce forest, which are wet and boggy, with some spur trails reaching into the alpine zone. Potential for mountain, glacier and wildlife viewing in alpine zone is outstanding. There are also some interesting lakes along the trail system. A seasonal ranger station is located near the southern end of Halibut Cove Lagoon.
U.S.G.S. Map:	Seldovia C-4.
Trail Begins:	Halibut Cove.
Condition Of Trail:	Minimal maintenance.
Other Trail Users:	None.
Agency Contact:	Alaska State Parks Morgan's Landing SRA P.O. Box 1247, Soldotna, AK 99669 Phone: Morgan's Landing, 907-262-5582; Homer Ranger Station, 907-235-7024
Boat Access:	From Homer to Halibut Cove. You must make own boat charter reservations through Central Charter Booking Agency at (907) 235-7847, or 800-478-7847 (in Alaska).
Season Of Use:	Summer.
Safety Concerns:	Crossing glacial streams, particularly in midsummer; hypothermia due to cold, wet weather; bears around camp and steep, rocky terrain above timberline.

WOSNESENSKI TRAIL (K-1A)

Length (one way):	2 miles.
Trip Time (one way):	One hour.
Degree of Difficulty:	Easy to moderate.
Elevation Gain:	-100 feet.
Unique Attractions:	Access to Wosnesenski River (a glacial river).
Trail Begins:	At end of China Poot Lake Trail.
Trail Ends:	Wosnesenski River.
Trail Facilities:	None.
Safety Concerns:	Glacial river crossing, hypothermia and black bears in your camp.

POOT PEAK TRAIL (K-1B)

Length (one way):	2 miles.
Trip Time (one way):	1.5-2 hours.
Degree of Difficulty:	Very difficult due to steep terrain.
Elevation Gain:	1,800 feet.
Unique Attractions:	Poot Peak and views of mountains and bay.
Trail Begins:	At terminus of China Poot Lake Trail.
Trail Ends:	At Poot PeakTrail.
Condition of Trail:	Unmaintained.
Trail Facilities:	None.
Safety Concerns:	Steep, rocky terrain and hypothermia.

CHINA POOT LAKE TRAIL (K-1C)

Length (one way):	2.5 miles.
Trip Time (one way):	1.3 hours.
Degree of Difficulty:	Easy.
Elevation Gain:	600 feet.
Unique Attractions:	China Poot Lake.
Trail Begins:	At the far south end of Halibut Cove Lagoon.
Trail Ends:	Near southern end of China Poot Lake, at the intersection with Poot Peak and Wosnesenski.
Trail Facilities:	Primitive campsites at China Poot Lake

and China Poot Lake trailhead.
Footbridge across inlet stream to lake.

Safety Concerns: Black bears in the camp.

LAGOON TRAIL (K-1D)

Length (one way):	5.5 miles.
Trip Time (one way):	3 hours.
Degree of Difficulty:	Moderate.
Elevation Gain:	1,200 feet.
Unique Attractions:	Connector trail to the alpine zone.
Trail Begins:	At three trailheads - Saddle Trail, Halibut Creek Trail and the quarter-mile China Poot Lake Trail.
Trail Ends:	Northeast side of Halibut Cove and the south end of Halibut Cove Lagoon.
Trail Facilities:	None.
Safety Concerns:	Black bears in the camp. Crossing Halibut Creek.

HALIBUT CREEK TRAIL (K-1E)

Length (one way):	1.5 miles.
Trip Time (one way):	1.2 hours.
Degree of Difficulty:	Easy to moderate.
Elevation Gain:	400 feet.
Unique Attractions:	A beautiful subalpine basin.
Area Description:	Trail ends in a subalpine basin surrounded by cliffs.
U.S.G.S. Map:	Seldovia C-4
Trail Begins:	At the southeast corner of Halibut Cove (not the lagoon) near the mouth of Halibut Creek.
Trail Ends:	At the head of Halibut Creek basin.
Condition of Trail:	Minimally maintained.
Trail Facilities:	None.
Season of Use:	Summer.
Safety Concerns:	Black bears in the camp.

GOAT ROPE TRAIL (K-1f)

Length (one way):	0.5 miles.
Trip Time (one way):	1 hour.
Degree of Difficulty:	Difficult.
Elevation Gain:	1,000 feet.
Unique Attractions:	View of mountains and bay. Wildflower displays.
Trail Begins:	At Halibut Creek or China Poot Lake trailheads. Picks up the Goat Rope Trail at the highest point on the Lagoon Trail.
Trail Ends:	At the alpine zone.
Trail Facilities:	None.
Safety Concerns:	Steep, rocky terrain.

ALPINE RIDGE TRAIL (K-1G)

Length (one way):	2 miles.
Trip Time (one way):	1.4 hours.
Degree of Difficulty:	Moderate.
Elevation Gain:	1,200 feet.
Unique Attractions:	View of mountains, Grewingk Glacier and a glacial valley.
Trail Begins:	After a quarter-mile on the Saddle Trail, turn south on Alpine Ridge Trail.
Trail Ends:	At the alpine zone.
Trail Facilities:	None.
Safety Concerns:	Steep terrain in alpine zone. Lack of well defined trail in the alpine zone; cairns mark that portion of the trail.

SADDLE TRAIL (K-1H)

Length (one way):	1 mile.
Trip Time (one way):	0.5 hours.
Degree of Difficulty:	Moderate.
Elevation Gain:	350 feet.
Unique Attractions:	Access to Grewingk Glacier.
Trail Begins:	At northeast corner of Halibut Cove. Mainly a connector trail to Grewingk Glacier Trail.

Trail Ends:	At the Grewingk Glacier Trail.
Trail Facilities:	None.
Safety Concerns:	Black bears in the camp.

GREWINGK GLACIER (K-11)

Length (one way):	3.5 miles.
Trip Time (one way):	1.5 hours.
Degree of Difficulty:	Easy.
Elevation Gain:	50 feet.
Unique Attractions:	Views of Grewingk Glacier and mountains. Trail winds through spruce and cottonwood and then across the outwash of the glacier. The outwash portion is marked by cairns.
Trail Begins:	On north side of Halibut Cove.
Trail Ends:	At the Grewingk Glacier Trail.
Trail Facilities:	Primitive campground on side trail about three-quarters of a mile from trailhead.
Safety Concerns:	Steep, rocky terrain near the glacier. Access to the glacial ice is hazardous due to a slide area on the south and steep cliffs on the north.

The Foothills of the Kenai Mountains.

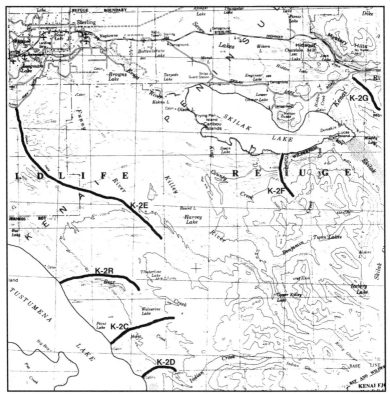

Map of trails away from Main Road System in Kenai National Wildlife Refuge

ROUTES WITH MINIMUM MAINTENANCE IN KENAI NATIONAL WILDLIFE REFUGE (K-2)

Unique Attractions:	Wildlife viewing and access to alpine zone (Kenai Mountains).
Area Description:	Trails pass through lowland spruce or spruce-birch forests. These are wet, boggy zones that are often rutted. Moose can be seen in low country; sheep, goat and caribou, in the high country. Outstanding views of the Kenai Mountains, glaciers and river valleys above timberline.
U.S.G.S. Map:	See individual trail.

Condition of Trails: Minimal maintenance.

Other Trail Users: Horseback riders in summer and fall; snowmobile users below timberline in winter.

Agency Contact: Kenai National Wildlife Refuge
Box 2139, Soldotna, AK 99669
Phone: (907) 262-7021

Season of Use: Summer/Fall.

Safety Concerns: High winds create dangerous lake crossings to reach some trailheads. Black bears in camp. Hypothermia, particularly above timberline. Storms, wind-chill factors and avalanches in winter. Difficulty in locating trail at timberline when returning. Mark trail temporarily before venturing above timberline.

DOC POLLARD HORSE TRAIL (K-2A)

Length (one way):   7 miles.

Trip Time (one way):   3 hours.

Degree of Difficulty: Easy to moderate.

Elevation Gain: 200 feet.

Unique Attractions: Access to Tustumena Lake and moose hunting.

U.S.G.S. Map: Kenai B-3, B-4.

Trail Begins: At 1.7 miles east of Sterling Highway. Turn off Mile 108.8 Sterling Highway to southeast. The Kalifonsky Beach Road turns northeast at that intersection. Continue straight for 1.7 miles where it intersects perpendicular with another road. The trail takes off directly across from the intersection. (Not on map.)

Trail Ends: Tustumena Lake.

Trail Facilities: Limited parking. No trailhead sign.

Safety Concerns: Sudden winds making Tustumena Lake dangerous boating. Bears in the camp.

BEAR CREEK TRAIL (K-2B)

Length (one way):	16.5 miles.
Trip Time (one way):	1.6 days.
Degree of Difficulty:	Moderate.
Elevation Gain:	3,000 feet.
Unique Attractions:	Access to alpine zone. Views of mountains.
U.S.G.S. Map:	Kenai A-2, A-3.
Trail Begins:	Boat access from Tustumena Campground to the mouth of Bear Creek. Trail parallels west side of creek.
Trail Ends:	In the alpine zone.
Trail Facilities:	None.
Safety Concerns:	Sudden winds making Tustumena Lake dangerous boating, bears in the camp and hypothermia.

MOOSE CREEK TRAIL (K-2C)

Length (one way):	7.7 miles.
Trip Time (one way):	4 hours.
Degree of Difficulty:	Moderate.
Elevation Gain:	2,500 feet.
Unique Attractions:	Access to alpine zone and views of mountains, glaciers and wildlife.
U.S.G.S. Map:	Kenai A-2.
Trail Begins:	Boat access from Tustumena Lake Campground towards the east end of the lake. Trail starts on west side of the mouth of Moose Creek.
Trail Ends:	Above timberline.
Trail Facilities:	None.
Safety Concerns:	Sudden winds making Tustumena Lake dangerous boating and bears in the camp.

LAKE EMMA TRAIL (K-2D)

Length (one way):	4.6 miles.
Trip Time (one way):	2.5 hours.
Degree of Difficulty:	Moderate to difficult.

Elevation Gain:	1,000 feet.
Unique Attractions:	Access to alpine zone. Views of mountains, glaciers and lake. Rainbow trout fishing.
U.S.G.S. Map:	Kenai A-2.
Trail Begins:	Boat access from the Tustumena Campground to the southeast arm of Tustemena Lake. Trail begins at lakeshore, a quarter-mile west of the mouth of Indian Creek.
Trail Ends:	At Lake Emma.
Trail Facilities:	Public-use cabin at Lake Emma. Free to use on a first-come, first-served basis. No firewood available. Must have backpack stove.
Safety Concerns:	Sudden winds making Tustumena Lake dangerous for boating. Bears in camp.

FUNNY RIVER HORSE TRAIL (K-2E)

Length (one way):	11 miles.
Trip Time (one way):	2 days.
Degree of Difficulty:	Not difficult, but travel is slow due to boggy conditions and downed trees.
Elevation Gain:	2,000 feet.
Unique Attractions:	Access to alpine zone and views of the mountains, alpine flora and wildlife.
U.S.G.S. Map:	Kenai B-2, B-3.
Trail Begins:	At Mile 7 of the Funny River Road. Turn east off of Sterling Highway at Mile 96 – a quarter-mile south of the Kenai River Bridge – onto Funny River Road. Then drive seven miles to the trailhead on south side of the road.
Trail Ends:	At the alpine zone.
Trail Facilities:	Trailhead sign and limited parking about a quarter-mile away.
Safety Concerns:	Brown bears along the horse trail, white-outs above timberline. Hypothermia.

COTTONWOOD CREEK TRAIL (K-2f)

Length (one way):	3.1 miles.
Trip Time (one way):	1.5 hours.
Degree of Difficulty:	Moderate to difficult.
Elevation Gain:	2,000 feet.
Unique Attractions:	Access to alpine zone and views of mountains, the lake and wildlife, potentially caribou and sheep.
U.S.G.S. Map:	Kenai B-1.
Trail Begins:	Boat access from the west end of Skilak Lake. Trail head is south past the end of the lake at the mouth of Cottonwood Creek.
Trail Ends:	About timberline.
Trail Facilities:	Public-use cabin at the lake. Use is on a first-come, first-served basis.
Safety Concerns:	Sudden winds making Skilak Lake dangerous for boating. Bears in the camp.

SURPRISE CREEK (K-2G)

Length (one way):	4.2 miles.
Trip Time (one way):	2.6 hours.
Degree of Difficulty:	Moderate to difficult. Steep and wet in places.
Elevation Gain:	2,200 feet.
Unique Attractions:	Alpine zone. Views of mountains, river valley and wildlife. Berry picking in late summer.
U.S.G.S. Map:	Kenai B-1.
Trail Begins:	Directly across the Kenai River from Jim's Landing Campground. River is very swift at that point.
Trail Ends:	At alpine zone, in the saddle near the headwaters of Surprise Creek.
Trail Facilities:	None.
Safety Concerns:	Swift water at Kenai River. Whiteouts above timberline where trail is undefined. Hypothermia. Bears in camp.

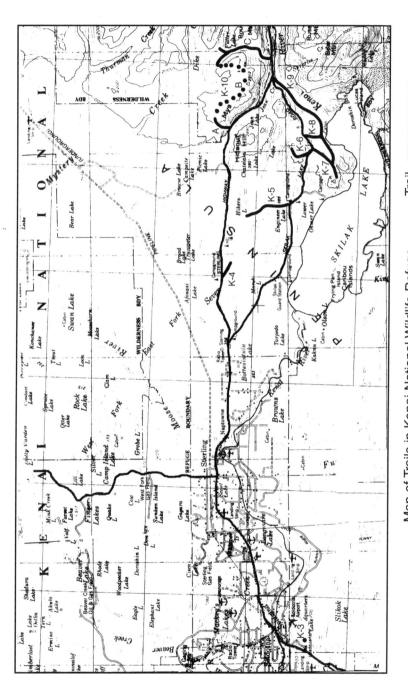

Map of Trails in Kenai National Wildlife Refuge
Associated with the Main Road System

Trail ———
Route •••••••••

MAINTAINED TRAILS IN THE KENAI NATIONAL WILDLIFE REFUGE

KEEN EYE TRAIL (K-3)

Length (one way):	0.5 miles.
Trip Time (one way):	0.5 hours.
Degree of Difficulty:	Easy.
Elevation Gain:	Minimal.
Unique Attractions:	Learn natural history of area.
Area Description:	A good example of the spruce forest ecosystem so prevalent on eastern portion of the Kenai Peninsula.
Trail Begins:	At refuge headquarters/visitor center. Turn east off the Sterling Hwy (a quarter-mile south of the Kenai River Bridge) onto Funny River Road. Immediately turn south on Ski Hill Road. Headquarters is one mile. Watch for sign.
Trail Ends:	At the visitor center.
Condition of Trail:	Maintained.
Trail Facilities:	Well-maintained trail with numbered markers keyed to a natural history brochure. Pick up your brochure at the visitor center.
Other Trail Users:	Cross-country skiers in winter, with an expanded trail system.
Agency Contact:	Kenai National Wildlife Refuge Box 2139, Soldotna, AK 99669 Phone: (907) 262-7021
Season of Use:	Summer.
Safety Concerns:	None.

EGUMEN LAKE TRAIL (K-4)

Length (one way):	0.6 miles.
Trip Time (one way):	0.4 hours.
Degree of Difficulty:	Easy.
Elevation Gain:	Minimal.

Unique Attractions:	Access to Egumen Lake. Limited fishing for rainbow trout.
Area Description:	New growth spruce forest, with interspersed bog areas.
U.S.G.S. Map:	Kenai C-2.
Trail Begins:	At Mile 70.4 of the Sterling Highway.
Trail Ends:	At Egumen Lake.
Condition of Trail:	Flat, maintained trail, may be wet.
Trail Facilities:	None.
Other Trail Users:	None.
Agency Contact:	Kenai National Wildlife Refuge Box 2139, Soldotna, AK 99669 Phone: (907) 262-7021
Season of Use:	Summer.
Safety Concerns:	Black bears around camp.

SEVEN LAKES TRAIL (K-5)

Length (one way):	5 miles.
Trip Time (one way):	2.5 hours.
Degree of Difficulty:	Easy.
Elevation Gain:	Minimal.
Unique Attractions:	Wildlife viewing around lakes. Trout fishing in Kelly, Engineer and Hidden Lakes.
Area Description:	Spruce bog zone. Excellent views of lake and mountains along the trail.
U.S.G.S. Map:	Kenai B-1, C-2, C-3.
Trail Begins:	At two trailheads – Kelly Lake (Mile 68.3 of the Sterling Highway) and Engineer Lake (Mile 9.6 of the Skilak Lake Road).
Condition of Trail:	Maintained. Wet and muddy from the spur trail to Hidden Lake to Engineer Lake.
Trail Facilities:	None.
Other Trail Users:	Good snowshoeing in winter.
Agency Contact:	Kenai National Wildlife Refuge Box 2139, Soldotna, AK 99669 Phone: (907) 262-7021
Season of Use:	Summer.
Safety Concerns:	Black bears around camp.

BEAR MOUNTAIN TRAIL (K-6)

Length (one way):	1.2 miles.
Trip Time (one way):	0.8 hours.
Degree of Difficulty:	Moderate.
Elevation Gain:	520 feet.
Unique Attractions:	Excellent views of Kenai Mountains and Skilak Lake. Good wildflower displays.
Area Description:	Trail passes spruce forest and then alder right below timberline. The top of the mountain is open, alpine tundra.
U.S.G.S. Map:	Kenai B-1
Trail Begins:	Mile 6.1 on Skilak Lake Road.
Trail Ends:	Above timberline, near top of Bear Mtn.
Condition of Trail:	Maintained. May be wet first part of trail.
Trail Facilities:	None.
Other Trail Users:	Snowshoers and cross-country skiers in winter.
Agency Contact:	Kenai National Wildlife Refuge Box 2139, Soldotna, AK 99669 Phone: (907) 262-7021
Season of Use:	Summer.
Safety Concerns:	Black bears and moose.

SKILAK LOOKOUT TRAIL (K-7)

Length (one way):	2.6 miles.
Trip Time (one way):	1.5 hours.
Degree of Difficulty:	Easy to moderate.
Elevation Gain:	750 feet.
Unique Attractions:	Excellent views of the Kenai Mountains and Skilak Lake. Good wildflower displays. Berry picking in late summer.
Area Description:	Trail passes through spruce and spruce-cottonwood forests to a knob overlooking the valley. The last portion of the trail is much steeper.
U.S.G.S. Map:	Kenai B-1.
Trail Begins:	At Mile 5.4 of the Skilak Lake Road.
Trail Ends:	At knob overlooking Skilak Lake.
Condition of Trail:	Maintained. Wet in low spots.

Trail Facilities:	None.
Other Trail Users:	Snowshoers. Not well suited to cross-country skiing.
Season of Use:	Summer.
Agency Contact:	Kenai National Wildlife Refuge Box 2139, Soldotna, AK 99669 Phone: (907) 262-7021
Safety Concerns:	Black bears and moose.

HIDDEN CREEK TRAIL (K-8)

Length (one way):	1.5 miles.
Trip Time (one way):	1 hour.
Degree of Difficulty:	Easy to moderate.
Elevation Gain:	-300 feet.
Unique Attractions:	Views of Skilak Lake and Kenai Mountains. Good wildlife viewing: moose, otter, eagles and waterfowl. Fair fishing.
Area Description:	Trail parallels Hidden Creek through spruce forest to Skilak Lake. Some good camping near the lake. Wild berries are often available in late summer.
U.S.G.S. Map:	Kenai B-1.
Trail Begins:	At Mile 4.5 of the Skilak Lake Road.
Trail Ends:	About one mile southwesterly of the point where trail emerges along lakeshore.
Condition of Trail:	Maintained. Generally dry.
Trail Facilities:	Footbridge across Hidden Creek had been washed out at time of writing. Thus, easterly trail has been eliminated.
Other Trail Users:	Cross-country skiers in winter.
Agency Contact:	Kenai National Wildlife Refuge Box 2139, Soldotna, AK 99669 Phone: (907) 262-7021
Season of Use:	Summer.
Safety Concerns:	Black bears and moose.

View of the Kenai River Canyon along the trail.

KENAI RIVER TRAIL (K-9)

Length (one way):	5.5 miles (2.3 miles on short loop).
Trip Time (one way):	3.6 hours (1.7 hours on short loop).
Degree of Difficulty:	Easy to moderate.
Elevation Gain:	- 600 feet.
Unique Attractions:	Access to the Kenai River. Scenic views of Kenai River Canyon on short loop. Wildlife viewing can be excellent.
Area Description:	There are two sections: (1) upper loop and (2) lower, a dead-end section. There

are a number of good camping spots along the river. Berry picking can be good in late summer.

U.S.G.S. Map:	Kenai B-1.
Trail Begins:	Two trailheads – Mile 0.7 and 2.4 on Skilak Lake Road.
Trail Ends:	Trail loops between the two trailheads and the westward extension terminates near the mouth of the Kenai River, where it enters Skilak Lake.
Condition of Trail:	Maintained. Generally dry.
Trail Facilities:	None.
Other Trail Users:	Snowshoers. Not well-suited for cross-country skiers.
Agency Contact:	Kenai National Wildlife Refuge P.O. Box 2139, Soldotna, AK 99669 Phone: (907) 262-7021
Season of Use:	Summer/fall.
Safety Concerns:	Steep canyon walls along the river. Black bears in the camp. Moose.

MYSTERY HILLS TRAIL SYSTEM (K-10)

Length (one way):	A. Skyline - 1.3 miles; B. Fuller Lakes - 4.6 miles; C. Mystery Hill - (connects between a and b above) 8 miles.
Trip Time (one way):	A. 1.5 hours; B. 3.5 hours; C. 6 hours.
Degree of Difficulty:	Very difficult.
Elevation Gain:	A. Skyline, 1,800 feet; B. Fuller Lakes, 1,400 feet; C. Mystery Hills, 1,400 feet.
Area Description:	Mystery Hills is an isolated group of steep hills north of the Sterling Highway between miles 57-61. The hills are dotted by a series of peaks above 3,000 feet. The views make it all worthwhile. Wildflower displays in midsummer and berry picking in late summer.
Unique Attractions:	Outstanding views of Kenai Mountains, midsummer wildflower displays and wildlife viewing, particularly Dall sheep.
U.S.G.S. Map:	Kenai B-1, C-1.

Trail Begins:	At two trailheads. I - Fuller Lakes starts at Mile 57.2 of the Sterling Hwy; 2 - Skyline starts at Mile 61 of the Sterling Highway. Both are on the north side of the highway.
Trail Ends:	Skyline and Fuller Lakes trails end about timberline. The Mystery Hills Route connects the two.
Condition of Trail:	Unmaintained. Skyline portion very steep.
Trail Facilities:	Parking and signs at both trailheads. The Skyline parking is on the opposite side of the Sterling Highway from the trailhead.
Other Trail Users:	None.
Agency Contact:	Kenai National Wildlife Refuge P.O. Box 2139, Soldotna, AK 99669 Phone: (907) 262-7021
Season of Use:	Summer.
Safety Concerns:	Steep, rocky terrain. Black bears in camp.

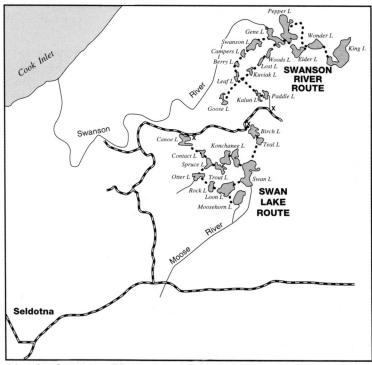

Map for Swanson River and Swan Lake Canoe Trails, Kenai
National Wildlife Refuge (X-denotes trailheads)
(●●●●●●● denotes portages)

SWANSON RIVER CANOE TRAIL SYSTEM (K-11)

Travel is slower than one might expect, but it is not difficult. Allow adequate time to enjoy the lakes, fishing and wildlife. Observe minimum impact camping. Campsites are available near the lakes, but are scarce along the Swanson River. Look for a well-drained site. With the exception of Wilderness and King, all lakes are closed to float planes.

ALTERNATE ROUTES & TRAVEL TIMES

Paddle Lake to Gene Lake . . . . 1-2 days
Gene Lake to Swanson River CG. . . . . . . 1-1½ days
   (Mile 18 on Swanson River Road)
Swanson River CG to Cook Inlet. . . . . . . 1-1½ days
   (add 1-1½ days for the Gene/Wonder/Lynx lakes Loop)

Area Description:	The trail is a series of lakes in the Kenai spruce lowlands connected via portages. Canoeists can return to entrance lake or float the Swanson River back to the road system. The region offers good fishing and moose hunting. Rainbow trout, Dolly Varden and red and silver salmon inhabit most lakes, but are lacking in Berry, Redpoll, Twig, Eider, Birchtree and Olsjold lakes. There are excellent bird-watching opportunities, particularly for loons.
U.S.G.S. Map:	Kenai C-2, C-3, D-2, & D-3
Trail Begins:	At Mile 12 of the Swan Lake Road. Turn north on Swanson River Road at Mile 83.7 of the Sterling Hwy – just west of Moose River Bridge. Then turn right on Swan Lake Road at Mile 17 of the Swanson River Road.
Trail Ends:	(1) Return to entrance, (2) take out at the end of Swanson River Road, or (3) take out at a service road off Mile 39, North

	Kenai Road (in the Captain Cook State Recreation Area).
Trail Facilities:	Portages between lakes, usually less than a half-mile apart. The portage between Swanson and Gene Lakes is longest at 1.1 miles.
Agency Contact:	Kenai National Wildlife Refuge P.O. Box 2139, Soldotna, AK 99669 Phone: (907) 262-7021
Other Trail Users:	None.
Season of Use:	Summer/fall.
Safety Concerns:	Black bear and brown bear in camp. Capsizing your canoe.

Canoeing in the Kenai National Wildlife Refuge.

SWAN LAKE CANOE TRAIL SYSTEM (K-12)

ALTERNATE ROUTES & TRAVEL TIMES

1. Swan Lake Road Return.
   a. Northern route (Gavia Lake) . . . .   2-3 days
   b. Southern route (Loon Lake). . . . .   2-3 days
2. Moose River Return.
   a. West/Camp Island Lake/Moose River Bridge
   . . . .   3-4 days
   b. East/Swan Lake/Moose River Bridge. . . . .   3-4 days

Area Description:	See Swanson River Canoe Trail System. Lakes void of fish are: Birch, Teal, Mallard, Raven, Otter and Big Mink.
U.S.G.S. Map:	Kenai C-2.
Agency Contact:	Kenai National Wildlife Refuge P.O. Box 2139, Soldotna, AK 99669 Phone: (907) 262-7021
Trail Begins:	West Entrance at Mile 3.9 of the Swan Lake Road and East Entrance at Mile 9.7 of the Swan Lake Road. See Swanson River Canoe Trail system for access to Swan Lake Road.
Trail Ends:	At either entrance or at the Moose River Bridge on the Sterling Highway.
Trail Facilities:	Portages between lakes, less than a half-mile.
Other Trail Users:	No.
Season of Use:	Summer/fall.
Safety Concerns:	Black and brown bear around the camp. Capsizing of your canoe.

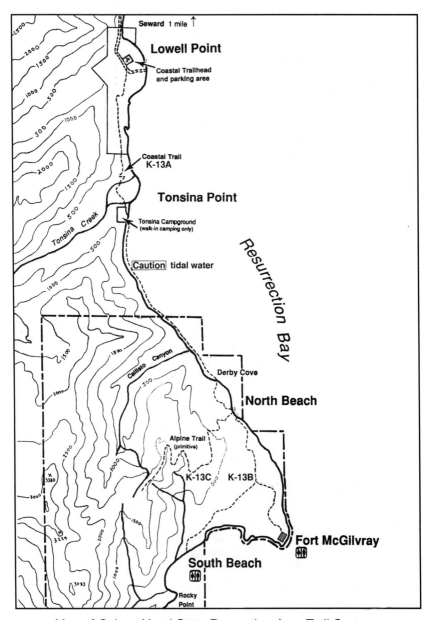

Map of Caines Head State Recreation Area Trail System

CAINES HEAD SRA TRAIL SYSTEM (K-13)

Degree of Difficulty:	Overall, easy to moderate, but difficult on the Alpine Trail segment.
Elevation Gain:	Minimal, except on the Alpine Trail.
Unique Attractions:	Historic Army post during World War II. Access to alpine zone. Outstanding views of Resurrection Bay.
Area Description:	Trail passes along Resurrection Bay shoreline from Lowell Point to South Beach. From Tonsina Point to North Beach you can travel only at low tide. There are footbridges across the creeks. Old ammunition magazines, platforms and piers mark the sites of interest.
U.S.G.S. Map:	Blying Sound D-7, Seward A-7.
Trail Begins:	At Lowell Point.
Trail Ends:	At South Beach.
Condition of Trail:	Minimal maintenance, uneven trail surface.
Trail Facilities:	Latrines, camping and picnic shelters and a ranger station.
Other Trail Users:	None.
Agency Contact:	Alaska State Parks P.O. Box 1247, Soldotna, AK 99669 Phone: (907) 262-5581
Season of Use:	Summer.
Safety Concerns:	Rising tide along coastal trail. Black bears in camp. Hypothermia due to cool, wet weather.

COASTAL TRAIL (K-13A)

Length (one way):	4.5 miles.
Trip Time (one way):	2.3 hours.
Trail Begins:	At Lowell Point (1 mile south of Seward waterfront).
Trail Ends:	At North Beach.
Trail Facilities:	Primitive campground with latrine and picnic shelter at both Tonsina Point and North Beach. Ranger station at North Beach.

The Coastal Trail at low tide along Resurrection Bay.

FORT McGILVRAY — SOUTH BEACH (K-13B)

Length (one way):	a. Fort McGilvray, 2 miles; b. South Beach, 2.5 miles.
Trip Time (one way):	a. 1 hour; b. 1.5 hours.
Degree of Difficulty:	Moderate to easy.
Elevation Gain:	650 feet.
Trail Begins:	At North Beach.
Trail Ends:	Two forks: (a) Fort McGilvray and (b) South Beach.
Trail Facilities:	Latrines at end of each fork.
Safety Concerns:	High cliffs surrounding Ft. McGilvray. Black bears in the camp.

ALPINE TRAIL (K-13C)

Length (one way):	2.2 miles.
Trip Time (one way):	1.6 hours.
Degree of Difficulty:	Difficult. Steep and rocky.
Elevation Gain:	1,800 feet.
Unique Attractions:	Alpine zone. Views of mountains and bay. Wildflower displays in midsummer.

Wildlife viewing – black bear and mountain goats.

Trail Begins: At North Beach.
Trail Ends: In alpine zone.
Trail Facilities: None.
Safety Concerns: Steep rocky terrain. Black bears in the camp.

MOUNT MARATHON TRAIL (K-14)

Length (one way):   1.5 miles.
Trip Time (one way):   2 hours.
Degree of Difficulty: Moderate to difficult (very steep on the last part).
Elevation Gain: 3,000 feet.
Unique Attractions: Views of mountains and Resurrection Bay. Wildlife viewing – ptarmigan, parka squirrels, black bear and mountain goats. Walk the trail that the marathoners run on July 4th.
Area Description: Trail starts in the spruce forest at the foot of the mountain, passing through forest and brush zones to timberline and on into the alpine zone. Trail is not well defined above timberline. The view from the top makes the hike worth it.
U.S.G.S. Map: Seward A-7.
Trail Begins: At the end of Monroe Street in Seward.
Trail Ends: In alpine zone.
Condition of Trail: Minimal maintenance. Generally dry, but can be wet and sloppy just after snow melt or long periods of rain.
Trail Facilities: Limited parking and trailhead sign.
Other Trail Users: No.
Season of Use: Summer.
Safety Concerns: Steepness of the trail. Black bears near the timberline.

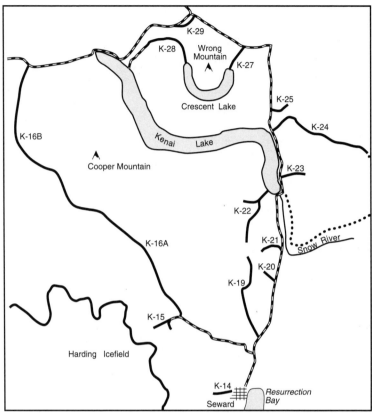

Map of Southern Kenai Trails, Chugach National Forest

EXIT GLACIER TRAIL SYSTEM (K-15)

Length (one way):	a. Interpretive Trail , 1.5 miles; b. Exit Glacier, 3.5 miles.
Trip Time (one way):	a. 1.5 hours; b. 2.5 hours.
Degree of Difficulty:	Easy (Interpretive trail); Moderate (Exit Glacier Trail).
Elevation Gain:	Minimal.
Unique Attractions:	Close up view of glacier. Wildlife, including mountain goats and black bears.
Area Description:	A unique, glacial-carved valley and an active glacier. One can view the valley

	from the Exit Glacier road, then up close from the trail system. The largest goat I have ever seen walked within 100 feet of me on the Interpretive Trail.
U.S.G.S. Map:	Seward A-7, A-8.
Trail Begins:	At Exit Glacier parking area. Turn west at Mile 3.4 on the Seward Highway onto Exit Glacier Road. Go nine miles to the parking area.
Trail Ends:	a. Interpretive Trail ends at the toe of the glacier; b. Exit Glacier Trail ends at Harding Icefield.
Condition of Trail:	Maintained. May be wet in spots.
Trail Facilities:	A half-mile paved portion of Interpretive Trail is suitable for the physically handicapped. Interpretive signs explain the history and dynamics of Exit Glacier. Some guided nature walks are available.
Other Trail Users:	No.
Agency Contact:	Kenai Fiord National Park P.O. Box 1727, Seward, AK 99664 Phone: (907) 224-3175
Season of Use:	Summer.
Safety Concerns:	Large pieces of falling ice around toe of the glacier. Watch for warning signs. Black bears.

RESURRECTION TRAIL SYSTEM (K-16)

Length (one way):	75 miles.
Trip Time (one way):	See individual segments.
Degree of Difficulty:	Easy to moderate.
Unique Attractions:	Historic overland trail. Outstanding scenery and wildlife viewing. Fishing available, primarily in the lakes. Public-use cabins available along trail.
Area Description:	The beginnings of the trail pass through dense spruce. Then, as the trail reaches higher country, many scenic vistas become visible. There is a variety of terrain, vegetation and wildlife along the

system. Most people use only a portion of the system; some do a new segment of the trail each year. A few hardy backpackers tackle it all at once. Even those can take a break and stock up on supplies where the trail crosses the Sterling Highway.

Trail Begins:	See individual trail segments.
Condition of Trail:	Well maintained, generally dry in high country. Wet and boggy in places in low country.
Trail Facilities:	Parking and entrance signs at trailheads. Footbridges across creeks and public-use cabins at varying intervals. Cabins may be rented six months in advance; $20 per night. Call (907) 224-3344 or 271-2599.
Other Trail Users:	Snowmobilers and cross-country skiers in winter (see individual trail segments), as well as horseback riders and mountain bikers.
Agency Contact:	Seward Ranger District U.S. Forest Service Box 390, Seward, AK 99664 Phone: (907) 224-3374
Season of Use:	Summer, fall and winter.
Safety Concerns:	Black bears in the camp and along Russian River during salmon runs. Failure to prepare for night on trail away from a cabin just because you have cabin reservations. Hypothermia, particularly during cool summer weather. Avalanches (see individual trail segments).

RESURRECTION RIVER TRAIL (K-16A)

Length (one way):	16 miles.
Trip Time (one way):	10 hours.
Degree of Difficulty:	Easy, except during wet weather.
Elevation Gain:	1,000 feet.
Unique Attractions:	Wildlife viewing, particularly for moose and bears. Mountain vistas.

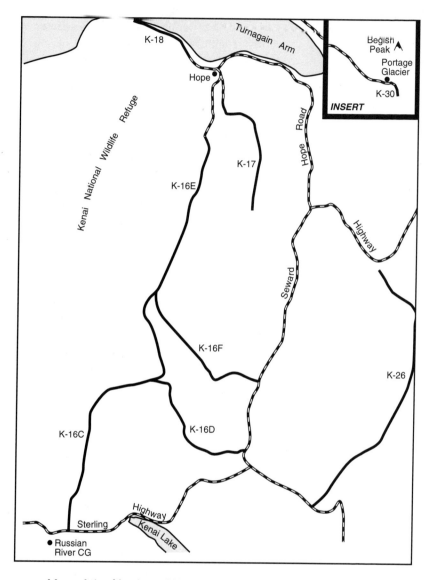

Map of the Northern Kenai Trails, Chugach National Forest

Area Description:	First eight miles are in dense spruce. Trail then climbs, offering some scenic vistas of the valley and mountains.
U.S.G.S. Map:	Seward A-7, A-8, B-8.

Trail Begins:	At end of Exit Glacier Road. Turn west at Mile 3.7 on Seward Highway onto Exit Glacier Road. It is 7.5 miles to the parking area.
Trail Ends:	At intersection with Russian Lakes Trail.
Condition of Trail:	Maintained. Wet in low spots.
Trail Facilities:	Large parking area at trailhead. Two metal bridges at Martin and Boulder creeks. Public-use cabin at Mile 6.5.
Other Trail Users:	Some cross-country skiers on first 6.5 miles to public-use cabin. However, Exit Glacier Road is not plowed beyond Mile 3, which may add significant time to reach the cabin. Horseback riders are welcome after June 30; snowmobiles from December 1 to April 30.
Season of Use:	Summer/fall.
Safety Concerns:	Black bears in the camp and along creeks during the summer. Hypothermia in fall and winter. Steep sidehilling, avalanches and distance makes this trail segment undesirable for winter travel, except to the cabin at Mile 6.5.

RUSSIAN LAKES TRAIL (K-16B)

Length (one way):	21 miles.
Trip Time (one way):	2.2 days.
Degree of Difficulty:	Easy.
Elevation Gain:	1,100 feet.
Unique Attractions:	Upper and Lower Russian lakes and wildlife viewing.
Area Description:	Both trails start in large spruce, then rise to elevations where good views open up. There are also opportunities to see wildlife, birds and spawning salmon up close. People may also use the trail for short day hikes out of the Russian River Campground. The Resurrection River Trail enters Russian Lakes Trail five miles from the Cooper Lake trailhead.

U.S.G.S. Map:	Seward B-8.
Trail Begins:	(1) Mile 1 of Russian River Campground Road, which exits south at Mile 52.8 on the Sterling Highway; (2) Mile 2.6 on the Cooper Lake Road. Turn southeast on Snug Harbor Road at Mile 48 of the Sterling Highway (near Kenai Lake outlet). Go 8.5 miles to Cooper Lake Road.
Condition of Trail:	Well maintained.
Trail Facilities:	Public-use cabins at Upper Russian Lake (12 miles from Russian River Campground), Aspen Flats (nine miles from Russian River Campground) and Lower Russian Lake (Barber cabin four miles from Russian River Campground).
Other Trail Users:	Horseback riders are welcome from July 1 through fall season. Snowmobilers from December 1 through February 15.
Season of Use:	Summer/fall.
Safety Concerns:	Black and brown bears on the Russian River. Winter storms and potential avalanches make trail from Russian River Campground Road to beyond the Lower Russian Lake unsafe for winter travel. Contact the U.S. Forest Service for winter travel information at (907) 224-3374.

RESURRECTION PASS TRAIL – SOUTH (K-16C)

Length (one way):	17.2 miles.
Trip Time (one way):	1.8 days.
Degree of Difficulty:	Moderate to easy.
Elevation Gain:	2,200 feet.
Unique Attractions:	Subalpine fishing lakes with public-use cabins. Midsummer wildflower displays and berry picking. Wildlife viewing opportunities. Specific points of interest are Juneau Falls (4.3 miles), Trout Lake (7 miles), Juneau Lake (9 miles) and Swan Lake (12.8 miles).
Area Description:	Trail begins in spruce-aspen forest and

	then rises through a transition zone to subalpine and alpine zones.
U.S.G.S. Map:	Seward B-8, C-8.
Trail Begins:	Mile 52.2 of the Sterling Hwy, north side, or the Bean Creek access from the end of Bean Creek Road (turn off at Mile 47.6 of the Sterling Highway). Bean Creek access is used more in the winter because of its uniform slope and straighter trail. Can also be accessed via Devil's Pass Trail, starting at Mile 39.4 of the Seward Highway.
Trail Ends:	Trail continues as Resurrection Pass Trail North, starting at Devil's Pass Trail junction.
Condition of Trail:	Well maintained. Wet in low spots.
Trail Facilities:	Parking and signs at trailheads. Public-use cabins are located at Trout Lake (7 miles), Romig (8.5 miles), Juneau Lake (9 miles), Swan Lake (12.8 miles) and Devil's Pass (17.2 miles). Footbridges.

➲ Note: There is a 1.5-mile hike from this trailhead across the Sterling Highway to the Russian Lakes trailhead. Walk 1 mile from the Russian Lakes trailhead to Sterling Highway and then left 0.5 miles to just south of Kenai River Bridge.

Other Trail Users:	Horseback riders are welcome between July 1 and the end of fall season. Snowmobiles are allowed from December 1 through February 15.
Season of Use:	Summer through fall and some winter use.
Safety Concerns:	Black bears in the camp. Hypothermia in fall and winter. Whiteouts in the winter.

DEVIL'S PASS TRAIL (K-16D)

Length (one way):	9.5 miles.
Trip Time (one way):	6 hours.
Degree of Difficulty:	Moderate to difficult.

Elevation Gain:	1,400 feet.
Unique Attractions:	Alpine zone. Wildflower displays, scenic views and wildlife – caribou, ptarmigan, marmot and possibly wolves.
Area Description:	Trail passes above timberline about three miles from trailhead. Good viewing opportunities of the alpine zone from Devil's Creek Canyon. Fishing for Dolly Varden at Devil's Pass Lake. With proper map and compass, cross-country travel is not difficult.
U.S.G.S. Map:	Seward C-7, C-8.
Trail Begins:	At parking lot at Mile 39.4 of the Seward Highway on the west side.
Trail Ends:	Intersection with Resurrection Pass Trail.
Condition of Trail:	Maintained. Dry.
Trail Facilities:	Devil's Pass cabin at the intersection, parking and sign at trailhead.
Other Trail Users:	Horseback riders between July 1 and end of the fall season. Snowmobilers are allowed between December 1 and February 15, but winter travel is hazardous and not recommended.
Season of Use:	Summer and fall.
Safety Concerns:	Black bears in the camp during summer. High avalanche potential in the winter.

RESURRECTION PASS TRAIL – NORTH (K-16E)

Length (one way):	21.4 miles.
Trip Time (one way):	2 days.
Degree of Difficulty:	Easy to moderate.
Elevation Gain:	2,100 feet.
Unique Attractions:	See K-16C.
Area Description:	See K-16C.
U.S.G.S. Map:	Seward C-8, D-8.
Trail Begins:	Mile 4 of Resurrection Creek Road. Take Hope Highway at Mile 56.3 of the Seward Highway. Turn left at Mile 15 of the Hope Highway onto Resurrection Creek Road.
Trail Ends:	Trail continues as Resurrection Pass Trail

	South from Devil's Pass Trail intersection.
Condition of Trail:	Well maintained. May be muddy in spots. Snow often persists into late June.
Trail Facilities:	Footbridges across creeks. Public-use cabins at Caribou Creek (7 miles*), Fox Creek (11.5 miles*) and East Creek (14.5 miles*). *Mileage from Hope Trailhead.
Other Trail Users:	Horseback riders are welcome from July 1 through fall season; snowmobilers from December 1 through February 15.
Season of Use:	All year.
Safety Concerns:	Black bears in camp during summer season. Hypothermia and storms during the fall and winter season. Whiteout conditions in winter.

SUMMIT CREEK TRAIL (K-16f)

Length (one way):	8.2 miles.
Trip Time (one way):	6 hours.
Degree of Difficulty:	Difficult.
Elevation Gain:	2,000 feet.
Unique Attractions:	Alpine zone. Wildflower displays in midsummer. Unique views of alpine valleys. Access to Resurrection Pass Trail.
Area Description:	Trail leads up 2,000 feet in first three miles to the alpine zone. Goes over two mountain passes.
U.S.G.S. Map:	Seward C-7, C-8.
Trail Begins:	At Mile 43.8 of the Seward Highway.
Trail Ends:	At Mile 19.5 of the Resurrection Pass Trail (measured from the Hope end).
Condition of Trail:	Not maintained. Dry, except near the beginning.
Trail Facilities:	None.
Other Trail Users:	Horseback riders are welcome from July 1 through the fall season.
Season of Use:	Summer and fall.
Safety Concerns:	Black bears in the camp during the summer. Steep, exhausting climb. High avalanche potential in winter.

PALMER CREEK TRAIL (K-17)

Length (one way):	6 miles.
Trip Time (one way):	2.5 hours.
Degree of Difficulty:	Easy to moderate.
Elevation Gain:	750-1,000 feet.
Unique Attractions:	Views of the alpine zone. The small, high mountain lakes (no fish). Midsummer wildflower displays.
Area Description:	Beautiful alpine zone. Turn west at Mile 56.5 of the Seward Highway onto Hope Highway. Drive 16.1 miles and turn left onto Resurrection Creek Road. In 0.7 miles, continue straight on Palmer Creek Road. Park at Coeur D'Alene Campground (Mile 7 of Palmer Creek Road). If this road is dry, you can drive slowly over the rough part beyond the campground. An old mining road turns left 4.5 miles beyond the campground. Follow it to where it bends sharply to the left to the Hershey Mine (about 0.4 of a mile). Park near old buildings. A path then goes straight over the ridge to Alder Creek (about another 0.6 miles). Two lakes lie at the headwaters of Alder Creek. Another trail leads from the old buildings (five miles from the campground) about 0.7 miles to a small waterfall.
U.S.G.S. Map:	Seward D-7.
Condition of Trail:	Not maintained. Dry.
Trail Facilities:	None.
Other Trail Users:	None.
Agency Contact:	Seward Ranger District U.S. Forest Service P.O. Box 390, Seward, AK 99664 Phone: (907) 224-3374
Season of Use:	Summer.
Safety Concerns:	Debris around the old mines.

GULL ROCK TRAIL (K-18)

Length (one way):	5.1 miles.
Trip Time (one way):	2.6 hours.
Degree of Difficulty:	Easy.
Elevation Gain:	600 feet.
Unique Attractions:	Scenic views of Turnagain Arm. Good family hike. Wildlife includes moose, black bear and beluga whale.
Area Description:	Trail passes through a variety of vegetation types while providing vistas of Turnagain Arm. On a clear day, you may even glimpse Mt. Denali. Trail follows an old wagon train road. Ruins of a sawmill, cabin and stable can be seen from Johnson Creek (near Gull Rock). Good berry picking in late summer.
U.S.G.S. Map:	Seward D-8.
Trail Begins:	At the northwest end of Porcupine Campground. At Mile 36.3 of the Seward Highway turn west onto Hope Highway, then drive 17.5 miles to the campground.
Trail Ends:	At Gull Rock.
Condition of Trail:	Well maintained, but wet and muddy in spots.
Trail Facilities:	None.
Other Trail Users:	None.
Agency Contact:	Seward Ranger District U.S. Forest Service P.O. Box 390, Seward, AK 99664 Phone: (907) 224-3374
Season of Use:	Summer.
Safety Concerns:	Tidal mud flats. The glacial mud can trap the unsuspecting hiker.

LOST LAKE (K-19)

Length (one way):	7 miles.
Trip Time (one way):	3 hours.
Degree of Difficulty:	Moderate to difficult.
Elevation Gain:	1,800 feet.

Unique Attractions:	Alpine zone, including Lost Lake. Rainbow trout fishing. Wildlife viewing — primarily mountain goats and black bears.
Area Description:	Alpine setting, nestled in a high basin surrounded by tall peaks and glaciers. Timberline is at Mile 5.5. Salmonberry patches can be found between Miles 4 and 5. First two-thirds of mile are now in private ownership and until access rights are resolved, enter via the Primrose Trail.
U.S.G.S. Map:	Seward A-7, B-7.
Trail Begins:	Trail begins at Mile 5 of the Seward Highway. Watch for sign.
Trail Ends:	At Lost Lake.
Condition of Trail:	Minimal maintenance.
Trail Facilities:	Footbridge over outlet to Lost Lake. Parking and sign at trailhead.
Other Trail Users:	Cross-country skiers and snowmobilers in winter.
Agency Contact:	Seward Ranger District U.S. Forest Service P.O. Box 390, Seward, AK 99664 Phone: (907) 224-3374
Season of Use:	All year.
Safety Concerns:	Hypothermia at any time of year. Whiteouts in winter.

GOLDEN FIN LAKE TRAIL (K-20)

Length (one way):	0.6 miles.
Trip Time (one way):	0.5 hours.
Degree of Difficulty:	Easy.
Elevation Gain:	100 feet.
Unique Attractions:	Subalpine lake setting.
Area Description:	Views of wet meadows and bog areas along trail. This is a good family hiking opportunity. Berry picking in late summer and skiing and sledding in winter.
U.S.G.S. Map:	Seward B-7.
Trail Begins:	At Mile 11.6 of the Seward Highway.
Trail Ends:	At Golden Fin Lake.

Condition of Trail:	Maintained. Can be very wet.
Trail Facilities:	Trail sign and parking.
Other Trail Users:	No.
Agency Contact:	Seward Ranger District
	U.S. Forest Service
	P.O. Box 390, Seward, AK 99664
	Phone: (907) 224-3374
Season of Use:	All year.
Safety Concerns:	Black bears. Hypothermia.

GRAYLING LAKE TRAIL (K-21)

Length (one way):	2 miles.
Trip Time (one way):	1.2 hours.
Degree of Difficulty:	Easy.
Elevation Gain:	450 feet.
Unique Attractions:	Subalpine lakes with grayling fishing.
Area Description:	There are three lakes on a bench above the Seward Highway accessed by three trails – Grayling, Meridan and Leech. All have grayling in them. Trail passes through spruce forests and mountain meadows. There are good low bush cranberries in late summer.
U.S.G.S. Map:	Seward B-7.
Trail Begins:	At Mile 13.2 of the Seward Highway. After about one mile, the trail forks – the left fork goes to Grayling Lake (a half-mile) and right fork goes to Meridan Lake (a quarter-mile). The half-mile trail to Leech Lake can be found along the east shore of Grayling Lake.
Trail Ends:	At the three lakes.
Condition of Trail:	Maintained. Wet in spots.
Trail Facilities:	Trail sign and parking.
Other Trail Users:	Cross-country skiers and snowshoers in winter. Also, snowmobilers welcome between December 1 and April 30 with adequate snow cover.
Agency Contact:	Seward Ranger District
	U.S. Forest Service

P.O. Box 390, Seward, AK 99664
Phone: (907) 224-3374

Season of Use: All year.
Safety Concerns: Black bears in the camp. Hypothermia
                            and whiteouts in the winter.

PRIMROSE TRAIL (K-22)

Length (one way):   7 miles (to Lost Lake).
Trip Time (one way):   4.5 hours.
Degree of Difficulty: Moderate to difficult.
Elevation Gain: 1,500 feet.
Unique Attractions: Subalpine setting. Views of mountains
                            and lakes. Rainbow trout fishing in Lost
                            Lake.
Area Description: This is a beautiful subalpine setting with
                            views of the surrounding mountains.
                            There is good potential wildlife viewing –
                            mountain goat, black bear, Dall sheep,
                            ptarmigan and spruce grouse. Rainbow
                            trout fishing in Lost Lake. At Mile 3 there
                            is a short but steep spur trail to Porcupine
                            Falls. The main trail is an old mining road
                            with many relics of the mining era along
                            the trail. An active mine can be seen at
                            Mile 3.75. At timberline, the two-mile route
                            to Lost Lake is marked with 4"x4" posts
                            for fog/whiteout conditions. Once the trail
                            touches Lost Lake, it parallels the eastern
                            portion of the lake until it crosses the
                            outlet. At that point it becomes the Lost
                            Lake Trail. For a view of Mt. Ascension
                            and the increased opportunity to see
                            black bear and mountain goats, walk
                            along the north edge of the lake, then a
                            short ways to the west, up the valley. For
                            a longer, cross-country adventure, follow
                            the westerly drainages to Cooper Lake.
                            The hiking is relatively easy, but good
                            compass and map skills are necessary.
U.S.G.S. Map: Seward B-7.

Trail Begins:	At Primrose Campground, 1.5 miles on the campground road from Mile 17.3 of the Seward Highway.
Trail Ends:	At Lost Lake outlet.
Condition of Trail:	Maintained. Good condition up to Mile 4, where it becomes a steep, eroded trail to timberline. Wet above timberline.
Trail Facilities:	Parking and trailhead sign. Footbridge over outlet stream.
Other Trail Users:	Cross-country skiers. Snowmobilers are welcome from December 1 through April 30. The miner with a permit may use a motorized vehicle all year to Mile 3.75.
Agency Contact:	Seward Ranger District U.S. Forest Service P.O. Box 390, Seward, AK 99664 Phone: (907) 224-3374
Season of Use:	All year.
Safety Concerns:	Black bear in the camp. Whiteouts and hypothermia.

VICTOR CREEK TRAIL (K-23)

Length (one way):	3 miles.
Trip Time (one way):	2 hours.
Degree of Difficulty:	Moderate to difficult.
Elevation Gain:	1,100 feet.
Unique Attractions:	View of the alpine zone. Flora displays in midsummer. Wildlife viewing – mountain goats and brown bear.
Area Description:	Victor Creek trail is in a narrow alpine valley. It offers excellent wildflower displays and mountain goat viewing. The first mile or so is very steep.
U.S.G.S. Map:	Seward B-7.
Trail Begins:	At Mile 19.7 of the Seward Highway.
Trail Ends:	About three miles up Victor Creek. It is another two difficult miles up the drainage to the toe of Mother Goose Glacier.
Condition of Trail:	Minimal maintenance. Steep and dry.
Trail Facilities:	Parking on west side and trail sign on

	east side of Seward Highway.
Other Trail Users:	None.
Agency Contact:	Seward Ranger District
	U.S. Forest Service
	P.O. Box 390, Seward, AK 99664
	Phone: (907) 224-3374
Season of Use:	Summer/fall.
Safety Concerns:	Brown bear in area. Steep terrain away from trail. Avalanche hazard eliminates winter use. In fact, avalanches often cover the trail through June, forcing summer use to start in July.

PTARMIGAN CREEK TRAIL (K-24)

Length (one way):	7.5 miles.
Trip Time (one way):	3 hours.
Degree of Difficulty:	Moderate. Snowy Pass route is difficult.
Elevation Gain:	450 feet (to upper part of Ptarmigan Lake); 1,200 feet (from lake to Snowy River Pass).
Unique Attractions:	Multiple destinations – Ptarmigan Lake, upper Ptarmigan Creek and a long distance trek over the Snowy River Pass to lower Paradise Lake.
Area Description:	Trail begins in the dense spruce forest, then rises to offer panoramic views. Ptarmigan Lake is at Mile 3.5 (1.5 hours). First two miles are moderately steep, then trail is level to the end of the lake. The longer trek over Snowy River Pass to Lower Paradise Lake has an alternate return route down the Snowy River drainage to the Seward Highway – about 30 miles total trip. There is an old trail at the foot of the mountains and a U.S. Forest Service public-use cabin at Lower Paradise Lake. Call (907) 224-3374 or 271-2599 for information and reservations. Grayling are found in the two lakes, with rainbow and Dolly Varden trout in

Ptarmigan Creek. Excellent wildlife viewing, particularly for mountain goats, Dall sheep, black bear and moose.

U.S.G.S. Map:	Seward B-6, B-7.
Trail Begins:	At Mile 23 of the Seward Highway.
Trail Ends:	At upper end of Ptarmigan Lake.
Condition of Trail:	Maintained. Wet in spots.
Trail Facilities:	Parking and trailhead sign.
Other Trail Users:	None.
Agency Contact:	Seward Ranger District
	U.S. Forest Service
	P.O. Box 390, Seward, AK 99664
	Phone: (907) 224-3374
Season of Use:	Summer and early fall.
Safety Concerns:	Black bears in the camp. Hypothermia and avalanche hazard in the winter. Plan your trip carefully for the long trek into Lower Paradise Lake.

VAGT LAKE (K-25)

Length (one way):	1.3 miles.
Trip Time (one way):	0.8 hours.
Degree of Difficulty:	Easy.
Elevation Gain:	150 feet.
Unique Attractions:	Fishing for rainbow trout in Vagt Lake.
Area Description:	Trail is located in the spruce forest. The destination is the lake. This is an easy family outing.
U.S.G.S. Map:	Seward B-7.
Trail Begins:	At the outlet to Lower Trail Lake. Turn off at Mile 25.1 of the Seward Highway. Cross railroad tracks and immediately turn left. Drive 0.2 miles to Lower Trail Lake. This trail follows shoreline for 0.5 miles before ascending to Vagt Lake.
Trail Ends:	At Vagt Lake.
Condition of Trail:	Not maintained. Wet in spots.
Trail Facilities:	Limited parking.
Other Trail Users:	None.
Agency Contact:	Seward Ranger District

U.S. Forest Service
P.O. Box 390, Seward, AK 99664
Phone: (907) 224-3374

Season of Use: Summer/fall.
Safety Concerns: Black bear.

JOHNSON PASS TRAIL (K-26)

Length (one way):   23 miles.
Trip Time (one way):   2.5 days.
Degree of Difficulty: Moderate to easy.
Elevation Gain: 1,000 feet.
Unique Attractions: Spectacular views of the mountains and
                         valleys. Good wildlife viewing
                         opportunities for moose, Dall sheep and
                         black bear. Trail follows part of the
                         Iditarod National Historic Trail.
Area Description: This is an excellent hiking opportunity for
                         those who prefer longer trips. The south
                         end of the trail meanders through spruce
                         forest and bog areas to within about 1.5
                         miles of Johnson Lake. For the next eight
                         miles the trail is in the alpine zone and
                         passes by two alpine lakes. Johnson Lake
                         has good fishing for rainbow trout; Bench
                         Lake, grayling. About four miles from the
                         north trailhead, the trail crosses a bridge
                         over Bench Creek and descends through
                         spruce forest.
U.S.G.S. Map: Seward C-7, C-7.
Trail Begins: South trailhead starts at Mile 32.5 of the
                         Seward Highway; the north trailhead at
                         Mile 64.
Trail Ends: Through route between the two trailheads.
Condition of Trail: Maintained. Wet in spots. Persisting snow.
Trail Facilities: Parking and trailhead signs. Footbridge
                         over Bench Creek.
Other Trail Users: Cross-country skiers on lower ends of
                         trail. Snowmobiling allowed between
                         December 1 and April 30 only on
                         lower south end. Horseback riders from

Season of Use:	July 1 through fall season. Summer and fall. Winter use limited to lower ends of the trail.
Safety Concerns:	Black bear. Avalanche hazard in winter in alpine zone.

CARTER LAKE TRAIL (K-27)

Length (one way):	3.3 miles.
Trip Time (one way):	2 hours.
Degree of Difficulty:	Difficult first 1.5 miles, then easy.
Elevation Gain:	100 feet.
Unique Attractions:	Views of the lakes and alpine zone. Good rainbow fishing in Carter Lake. Marginal grayling and Dolly Varden fishing at the east end of Crescent Lake. Beautiful alpine floral displays.
Area Description:	The vegetation opens up near Carter Lake, giving spectacular views of the alpine zone. Trail becomes less distinct the last three-quarters of a mile beyond Carter Lake to Crescent Lake. The steep terrain on both sides of Crescent Lake makes travel to the west end of lake extremely difficult and hazardous.
U.S.G.S. Map:	Seward B-7, C-7.
Trail Begins:	At Mile 34 of the Seward Highway.
Trail Ends:	At east end of Crescent Lake. However, a primitive trail loops around the south side of the lake to the Crescent Creek Trail.
Condition of Trail:	Maintained. Wet above timberline.
Trail Facilities:	Parking and trailhead sign.
Other Trail Users:	Difficult for cross-country skiers because of steep start. Snowmobilers allowed December 1 through April 30. Horseback riders from July 1 to end of fall season.
Agency Contact:	Seward Ranger District U.S. Forest Service P.O. Box 390, Seward, AK 99664 Phone: (907)224-3374
Season of Use:	All year, with caution in winter.

Safety Concerns: Black bear in the camp. Hypothermia and avalanche hazard away from trail in high country in fall and winter.

CRESCENT CREEK TRAIL (K-28)

Length (one way):   6.5 miles.
Trip Time (one way):   3.5 hours.
Degree of Difficulty: Moderate to easy.
Elevation Gain: 900 feet.
Unique Attractions: Crescent Lake. Wildflower displays. Wildlife viewing – black bear and Dall sheep. Grayling fishing.
Area Description: Trail ascends through birch-aspen forest over a ridge and then into Crescent Creek Canyon at Mile 1.2. From there to the lake is a gradual uphill climb through clusters of trees and open meadows. There are midsummer wildflower displays in the meadows, as well as periodic views of the alpine zone. Black bear may be seen in the transition zone, particularly in late summer. Dall sheep may be seen in the high country. Crescent Lake public-use cabin is situated right at the lake. There is good grayling fishing near the outlet of Crescent Lake and in Crescent Creek.
U.S.G.S. Map: Seward B-7, C-7, C-8.
Trail Begins: At Mile 3.5 Quartz Creek Road. Turn onto Quartz Creek Road at Mile 45 of the Sterling Highway. Drive past Quartz Creek and Crescent Creek campgrounds.
Trail Ends: At Crescent Lake; however, a primitive trail continues around the south side of the lake to the Crescent Saddle public cabin and to the Carter Lake Trail.
Condition of Trail: Maintained, but wet and muddy in spots.
Trail Facilities: Parking and trailhead sign. Bridge across Crescent Creek. Crescent Lake and Crescent Saddle public-use cabins are available for $20 per night. For

reservations call the U.S. Forest Service at (907) 224-3374 or 271-2599.

Other Trail Users: Horseback riders welcome from July 1 through end of fall season. Miners with permit may use motorized vehicles on trail.

Agency Contact: Seward Ranger District
U.S. Forest Service
P.O. Box 390, Seward, AK 99664
Phone: (907) 224-3374

Season of Use: Summer/fall.

Safety Concerns: Black bear in camp throughout the summer. High potential avalanche danger in winter and spring preclude travel during that time.

OLD STERLING HIGHWAY TRAIL (K-29)

Length (one way): 5.7 miles.

Trip Time (one way): 2.5 hours.

Degree of Difficulty: Easy.

Elevation Gain: Minimal.

Unique Attractions: Easy family hiking near campgrounds.

Area Description: Trail stays in spruce bottom between Tern Lake Campground and Crescent Creek trailhead. Some Dolly Varden fishing in Daves Creek.

U.S.G.S. Map: Seward B-8, C-7, C-8.

Trail Begins: At Mile 37.5 of Sterling Highway (Tern Lake Campground) and at Mile 3.5 of the Quartz Creek Road. Turn onto Quartz Creek Road at Mile 45 of the Sterling Highway.

Trail Ends: Loops between two trailheads.

Condition of Trail: Old highway. Not maintained.

Trail Facilities: None.

Other Trail Users: Occasional four-wheel-drive vehicles.

Agency Contact: Seward Ranger District
U.S. Forest Service
P.O. Box 390, Seward, AK 99664
Phone: (907) 224-3374

Season of Use: Summer/fall.
Safety Concerns: Black bear along Daves Creek.

BYRON GLACIER TRAIL (K-30)

Length (one way):   I mile.
Trip Time (one way):   0.5 hours.
Degree of Difficulty: Easy.
Elevation Gain: 100 feet.
Unique Attractions: View of Byron Peak and glacier.
Area Description: Trail leads to a small glacial valley and a
                        permanent snowfield below the glacier.
                        You can travel across the compacted
                        snow to the glacier, but stay away from
                        glacier and overhanging ice.
U.S.G.S. Map: Seward D-5.
Trail Begins: Near the end of the Portage Glacier Road
                        about one mile from the lodge. Portage
                        Glacier Road connects to the Seward
                        Highway at Mile 78.8.
Trail Ends: Near Byron Glacier.
Condition of Trail: Maintained.
Trail Facilities: Parking and trailhead sign.
Other Trail Users: None.
Agency Contact: Glacier Ranger District
                        U.S. Forest Service
                        P.O. Box 129, Girdwood, AK 99587
                        Phone: (907) 783-3242
Season of Use: Year round.
Safety Concerns: Traversing the glacier. This should only
                        be done by experienced and properly
                        equipped glacier climbers or groups
                        supervised by such people.

CABINS

Permits are issued for non-commercial purposes to anyone 18 years of age (or older) on a first-come, first-served basis. A permit day begins at 12 noon on the assigned day and ends at 12 noon the following day. When there is more than one application for the same cabin on the first day, permits will be awarded by a drawing. Reservations for the use of recreation cabins in the national forests of Alaska may be initiated a maximum of 179 days in advance of the first day of planned use. However, applications for permits may be postmarked or delivered in person up to 190 days before the first day of planned use. If there is more than one application for a given cabin, awarded by a drawing at 8 a.m. on the 179th day preceding the time of use. From May 15 through August 31, permits for hike-in cabins located along Resurrection Pass, Russian Lakes, Crescent Lake and Crow Pass trails are issued for a maximum stay of three consecutive nights; the maximum stay at all other cabins in the Forest is seven consecutive nights.

The cost is $20 a day, paid in cash, check or postal money order payable to USDA Forest Service. For all mail applications or for applications in advance of the 180th day, send only check or money order.

Cabin reservations may be made by mail or in person between the hours of 8 a.m. and 4:30 p.m. at the following address:

USDA Forest Service
Chugach National Forest
201 East 9th Avenue, Suite 206
Anchorage, AK 99501-3698

Cabin reservation information: (907) 271-2599.

Cabin reservations may be made in person at any of the following Chugach National Forest offices:

USDA Forest Service
Glacier Ranger District
P.O. Box 129
Girdwood, AK 99587-0129

USDA Forest Service
Seward Ranger District
334 Fourth Avenue
Seward, AK 99664-0390

The Forest Service provides boats and other cabin-related equipment at many cabins. However, the Forest Service cannot guarantee that these items will be in a serviceable condition or even available at all times. Refunds are not made if this equipment is not serviceable or available.

Boat users must provide an approved U.S. Coast Guard floatation device for each passenger. A small outboard motor (2-7.5 horsepower) may add to your enjoyment. Copies of fishing and hunting regulations may be obtained from:

Alaska Department of Fish and Game (ADF&G)
333 Raspberry Road
Anchorage, AK 99518

Cabins do not have electricity, bedding, or cooking utensil. Take a gas or propane stove for cooking, insect repellent and an air mattress or pad. Forest cabins do have outdoor sanitary facilities; some have an axe, saw and broom.

Drinking water is not provided. Water taken from lakes or streams should be boiled at least five minutes to make it safe for drinking.

Visitors should be prepared to gather firewood within the vicinity of the cabins. Where oil stoves are provided, No. I stove oil is recommended; five gallons will last allow 48 hours of continuous summer use – less in winter.

Cabin users are requested t comply with the following:
♦ Burn combustible waste
♦ Pack-out all other garbage, including unused food and fuel.
♦ Pack-out empty fuel cans and leave a supply of firewood.
♦ Not to cut live trees.

➲   Aircraft Services. Charter aircraft services are available in almost all Alaskan communities, including Anchorage, Cooper Landing, Cordova, Kenai, Moose Pass, Seward, Soldotna and Valdez. Aircraft services are generally listed in the yellow pages of local telephone books.

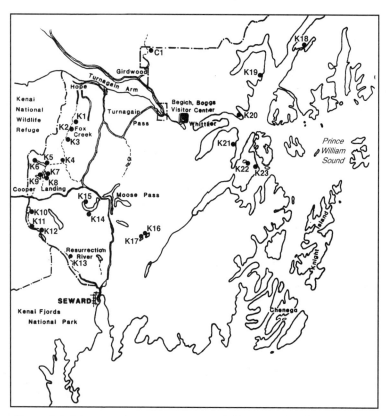

Map of Cabins on the western part of Chugach National Forest.
(Numbers refer to cabin descriptions on succeeding pages.)

The following is a list of available cabins in the Kenai-Eastern Prince
William Sound Area: All cabins are 12 x 14 feet unless indicated
otherwise.

K1. Caribou Creek – A cabin located in the Kenai Mountains.
Accessible via Resurrection Pass Trail (7.1 miles from the north
trailhead). Bunks six; wood stove. Local wildlife includes moose, black
bear, brown bear, sheep, wolves and goats.

K2. Fox Creek – Another cabin in the Kenai Mountains. Accessible via
Resurrection Pass Trail (12.5 miles from the north trailhead). Bunks

six; wood stove. Wildlife includes moose, black bear, brown bear, sheep and wolves.

K3. East Creek – Cabin in the Kenai Mountains. Accessible via Resurrection Pass Trail (14.4 miles from the north trailhead). Bunks six; wood stove. Wildlife includes moose, black bear, brown bear, sheep, caribou and wolves.

K4. Devil's Pass – An A-frame cabin, with loft, in the Kenai Mountains. Accessible via Resurrection Pass Trail (17.1 miles from the south trailhead) or via Devil's Pass Trail (10 miles from trailhead). Bunks six (sleeps 10); oil stove. No firewood available. Wildlife includes moose, black bear, brown bear, sheep, caribou and wolves.

K5. Swan Lake – Cabin in the Kenai Mountains. Accessible via Resurrection Pass Trail (13 miles from south trailhead) or via floatplane (30 minutes from Moose Pass; 15 minutes from Cooper Landing). Bunks six; wood stove. Wildlife includes moose, black bear, brown bear, caribou and wolves. Lake trout, rainbow trout and freshwater salmon fishing. Boat provided. During high-use periods in late August and early September, cabin must be reserved through special drawings.

K6. West Swan Lake – Cabin in the Kenai Mountains. Accessible via floatplane (30 minutes from Moose Pass; 15 minutes from Cooper Landing). Bunks six; wood stove. Wildlife includes moose, black bear, brown bear, caribou and wolves. Lake trout, rainbow trout and freshwater salmon fishing. Boat provided. During late August and early September, cabin must be reserved through special drawings.

K7. Juneau Lake – Cabin in the Kenai Mountains. Accessible via Resurrection Pass Trail (10 miles from the south trailhead) or via floatplane (20 minutes from Moose Pass; 10 minutes from Cooper Landing). Bunks six; wood stove. Wildlife includes moose, black bear, brown bear and wolves. Lake trout, rainbow trout, grayling and burbot fishing. Boat provided. During high-use periods in late August and early September, cabin must be reserved through special drawings.

K8. Rooming – Cabin located in the Kenai Mountains at the south end of Juneau Lake. Accessible via Resurrection Pass Trail (nine miles from south trailhead) or via floatplane (10 minutes from Cooper Landing). Bunks six; wood stove. Wildlife includes moose, black bear, brown bear, sheep and wolves. Lake trout, rainbow trout, grayling and burbot fishing. Boat provided. During high-use periods in late August and early September, cabin must be reserved through special drawings.

K9. Trout Lake – An A-frame cabin with loft in the Kenai Mountains. Accessible via Resurrection Trail (seven miles from south trailhead) or via floatplane (10 minutes from Cooper Landing). Bunks six (sleeps 10); wood stove. Wildlife includes moose, black bear, brown bear, sheep and wolves. Lake trout and rainbow trout fishing. Boat provided. During late August and early September cabin must be reserved through special drawings.

K10. Barber – A 16x20-foot log cabin in the Kenai Mountains. Accessible via Russian Lakes Trail (four miles from trailhead) or via floatplane (25 minutes from Seward; 22 minutes from Cooper Landing). Bunks five; wood stove. Handicapped accessible features: ramps at front and rear doors. Large pit toilets, boat and floatplane dock. Wildlife includes moose, black bear, brown bear and wolves. Rainbow trout fishing. Boat provided.

The Barber Cabin, Lower Russian Lake, Chugach National Forest.

K11. Aspen Flats – Cabin in the Kenai Mountains. Accessible via Russian Lakes Trail (nine miles from trailhead). Bunks six; wood stove. Wildlife includes moose, black bear, brown bear and wolves. Rainbow trout, Dolly Varden fishing in Upper Russian River.

K.12. Upper Russian Lake – A rustic log cabin in the Kenai Mountains. Accessible via Russian Lakes Trail (12 miles from Russian River Campground parking area) or via floatplane (20 minutes from Seward or Cooper Landing). Bunks four; wood stove. Wildlife includes moose, black bear, brown bear, sheep and wolves. Rainbow trout fishing. Boat provided.

K13. Resurrection River Trail – Cabin on the Resurrection River Trail (between Martin and Boulder creeks), three-quarters of a mile downstream from river's confluence with Boulder Creek. Accessible via Resurrection River Trail (6.5 miles from trailhead on Exit Glacier Road). Bunks six; wood stove. Wildlife includes moose, black bear, brown bear and sheep.

K14. Crescent Saddle - Cabin on the south shore of Crescent Lake. Accessible by trail (ll miles from the Crescent Lake Trailhead and 7.5 miles from the Carter Lake trailhead), or by floatplane. Season of use is primarily summer and fall. Boat provided. Excellent wildlife viewing and grayling fishing.

K15. Crescent Lake – Cabin in the Kenai Mountains. Accessible via Crescent Creek Trail (6.2 miles from parking area) or via floatplane (15 minutes from Moose Pass; 20 minutes from Cooper Landing). Crescent Lake cabin is inaccessible from Carter Lake Trail. Bunks six; wood stove. Wildlife includes moose, black bear, brown bear and sheep. Grayling fishing in lake (check with ADF&G for special regulations). No Forest Service boat provided.

K16. Upper Paradise Lake – Cabin located in the Kenai Mountains. Accessible via floatplane (15 minutes from Moose Pass; 25 minutes from Seward). Bunks six, wood stove. Wildlife includes moose, black bear, brown bear and goats. Grayling fishing. Boat provided.

K17. Lower Paradise Lake – Cabin in the Kenai Mountains. Accessible via floatplane (15 minutes from Moose Pass; 20 minutes from Seward). Bunks six, wood stove. Wildlife includes moose, black bear, brown bear and goats. Grayling fishing. Boat provided.

K18. Coghill Lake – An A-frame cabin, with loft, located at small lagoon on Coghill Lake in Upper Prince William Sound. Accessible via floatplane (50 minutes from Anchorage). Bunks six (sleeps 10); wood stove. Wildlife includes black bear. Salmon fishing. An inflatable boat may add to your enjoyment at this cabin; no Forest Service boat provided.

K19. Harrison Lagoon – A 16x20 foot cabin on the west side of Port Wells about 34 miles via boat from Whittier. Bunks five; wood stove. Drinking water accessible only via boat; carry initial supply of water. Wildlife includes black bear. Lagoon drains nearly dry when tides are low.

K20. Pigot Bay – An A-frame cabin, with loft, in the Prince William Sound area. Accessible via floatplane (40 minutes from Anchorage) or via boat (20 miles from Whittier). Bunks six (sleeps 10); wood stove. Drinking water is sometimes difficult to obtain near the cabin; carry initial supply of water. Wildlife includes black bear. Crabbing, saltwater and freshwater salmon fishing.

K21. Paulson Bay – A cabin on the west side of Cochrane Bay. Accessible via boat (17.5 miles from Whittier) or via floatplane (40 minutes from Anchorage). Bunks six, wood stove. Wildlife includes black bear. Crabbing, saltwater and freshwater salmon fishing.

K22. Shrode Lake – An A-frame cabin, with loft, in the Prince William Sound area. Accessible via boat (24 miles from Whittier) and semi-primitive hiking trail approximately one mile long or via floatplane (35 minutes from Seward; 45 minutes from Anchorage). Bunks six (sleeps 10); oil heater. Wildlife includes black bear. Dolly Varden in the lake and salmon fishing in the stream. Boat provided. Cabin usually not available until mid-June due to ice and snow conditions.

K23. South Culross Pass – Cabin on the west side of the south end of Culross Passage. Accessible via floatplane (45 minutes from Anchorage) or via boat (27 miles from Whittier). Inner lagoon is dry at low tide. Anchor large boats in outer bay and walk to cabin via route along north shore of inner lagoon. Bunks six; wood stove. Wildlife includes black bear. Crabbing, saltwater and freshwater salmon fishing.

KENAI NATIONAL WILDLIFE REFUGE

The cabin policy on the refuge is on a first-come, first-served basis. There is no charge for these cabins and the rules are simple.

- Pack out all trash.
- Clean the cabin and sweep the floor.
- For firewood, gather only dead and down wood at least a quarter-mile from cabin.
- Clean and dry any permanent pots, pans or dishes.
- Do not leave food.
- Close all shutters and secure door before you leave.
- Report any problems to the headquarters at Soldotna.

K24. BIG INDIAN CABIN

Location:	Kenai T9N, R4W, Section 4, NW ¼ Seward. NW end of Big Indian Airstrip.
Access:	Wheel aircraft on Big Indian Airstrip, four-wheel-drive vehicle from September 1 to October 20 and snowmachine.
Construction:	Plywood floor, 12x16 metal roof. One 4x4 frame outhouse.
Condition:	Cabin could use some maintenance, but is generally in good condition and has operable stove.
Accommodates:	4 to 6 persons.
Local Recreation:	Chickaloon estuary for waterfowl and big game hunting, and fishing for salmon.
Hazards:	Brown bears frequent the area.
Firewood:	Abundant.
Public Use:	Visitor days are 150-200 per year, primarily from September 1 through October 20.

K25. CARIBOU ISLAND

Location:	Kenai A-3, T2N, R10W, Section 29, NW ¼.
Access:	Primary access to this cabin is by powerboat, floatplane and snowmachine.
Construction:	Log, with an enclosed loft above. The roof is made of corrugated metal roofing over a 2x4 frame. The floor is made of hardboard/plywood. New toilet constructed in 1989. Received minor refuge maintenance.
Condition:	The log walls, roof and floor are in fair to good condition.

Accommodates:	4 persons.
Local Recreation:	Hunting and fishing in Nicolai Creek.
Hazards:	The shore is exposed to southerly winds; large waves could swamp boats not pulled out on the beach. There is little beach area available during high water.
Firewood:	Wood supply is poor. What little wood is available is mostly rotten birch.
Public Use:	Most popular Tustumena Lake shelter with 110-150 visitor days per year (20% during winter).

K26. CHICKALOON RIVER #1

Location:	Kenai D-1, T9N, R7W, Section 8, SE ¼.
Access:	Float- or wheelplane or boat from Hope or Chickaloon River.
Construction:	Plywood frame and a good roof. Built on stilts with entrance steps. Approximately 12x16-foot plywood floor. Oil stove.
Condition:	Fair to good.
Accommodates:	4 persons.
Local Recreation:	Waterfowl hunting.
Hazards:	Wheel plane landing requires skilled off-airport pilot. Floatplane landing requires careful negotiation of Lower Chickaloon River tides and dealing with severe waves.
Firewood:	Unavailable.
Public Use:	Cabin is used during waterfowl season by hunters; 50-100 visitor days per year.

K27. DOROSHIN BAY

Location:	Kenai B-1, T4N, R52, Section 22, NW ¼.
Access:	Primary access to this cabin is by powerboat with minimal floatplane access.
Construction:	Unpeeled logs with a new tarpaper, batten roof. The floor is built on rough-cut planks. Cabin has received maintenance from refuge in last several years and has new windows which improve lighting. Also has new outhouse.
Condition:	The cabin is in fair to good condition,

although major work is needed on the floor, roof and walls.

Accommodates:	4 persons.
Local Recreation:	Fishing is available nearby at the mouth of the Kenai River, as is waterfowl hunting. The Kenai River is two miles from the cabin. Big and small game hunting is available in the Skilak Flats.
Hazards:	Large, submerged rocks near shore present a hazard to approaching boats and floatplanes. Mosquitoes and whitesocks, though not a serious hazard, are bothersome and numerous due to the cabin's close proximity to a marsh.
Firewood:	Wood is available (mostly spruce), but is limited. Increased use of the cabin would rapidly deplete the wood supply near the cabin.
Public Use:	100-200 visitor days per year.

K28. FINGER LAKES CABIN

Location:	Kenai C-3, T7N, R9W, SW ¼.
Access:	The cabin is accessible by foot from Swanson River Road via the Finger Lakes Trail (road), by floatplane or snowmachine.
Construction:	Log, with a plywood floor. The roof is three-quarter-inch plywood covered with heavy asphalt roofing. Good stove.
Condition:	The cabin is in fair to good condition.
Accommodates:	4 persons.
Local Recreation:	Rainbow trout fishing is available in the lakes. Moose, bear and small game hunting are possible in the area.
Hazards:	None.
Firewood:	Available.
Public Use:	Most heavily used cabin due to easy access from the road. Approximately 300 visitor days per year.

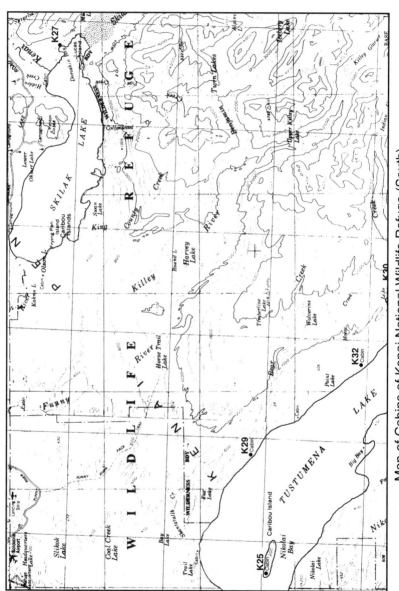

Map of Cabins of Kenai National Wildlife Refuge (South)

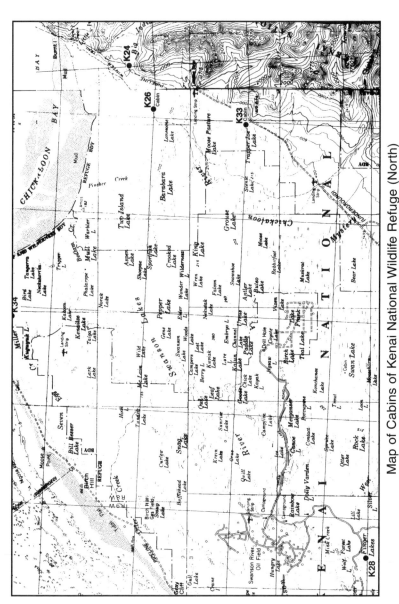

Map of Cabins of Kenai National Wildlife Refuge (North)
(Numbers refer to cabin descriptions on the succeeding pages)

K29. FRENCHIES CABIN

Location:	Kenai B-3, T2N, R10W, Section 3, NW ¼ (Tustumena Lake).
Access:	Primary access to this cabin is by powerboat, floatplane, snowmachine or horse.
Construction:	The cabin in constructed of dovetail connected logs. There is an enclosed loft above and open porch on the front of the cabin. The floor is three-quarter-inch plywood and the roof is corrugated metal. The cabin is well lit by five large windows. Cabin has been occasionally maintained by users.
Condition:	The cabin is in fair condition. Most logs are sound, though some base logs are beginning to decay.
Accommodates:	4 persons.
Local Recreation:	Hunting and fishing.
Hazards:	The shore is exposed to southerly winds, which cause large, breaking waves on the beach. During high water, there is not enough beach to permit haul-outs. Boats could easily become swamped.
Firewood:	Wood is available, but not abundant.
Public Use:	50-100 visitor days per year. Cabin is used as a stopover for up-lake boaters, those with snowmachines and hunters.

K30. LAKE EMMA CABIN

Location:	Kenai A-2, T1S, R7W, Section 6, NW ¼.
Access:	This cabin is reached by hiking from Tustumena Lake on the Lake Emma Trail or from trails heading to Marmot Pass. Motorized access by snowmachine is possible, but difficult. Floatplane landing on Lake Emma is prohibited.
Construction:	Construction is log, with sawn and hewn planks for the roof and floor. The roof planks are covered with thin plywood, tarpaper and hand-split shakes. Interior walls are well chinked and covered with

slats. A large enclosed porch is attached to one end of the cabin. The foundation is built on large rocks and it is likely that the base logs will not rot. Cabin has received regular maintenance from refuge.

Condition:	Good.
Accommodates:	2 persons.
Local Recreation:	The cabin is an access point to alpine high country where moose, sheep, bear, goats and other animals can be hunted. Lake Emma trailhead is located on Tustumena Lake.
Hazards:	Brown and black bears are common.
Firewood:	There is virtually no dead and down wood available within the immediate vicinity of the cabin. The wood supply has already been depleted. Coal stove.
Public Use:	Use occurs primarily during spring and fall for bear, sheep and moose seasons with light use in summer. Some winter use occurs. Trappers use cabin intermittently. 150-200 visitor days per year.

K31. THE NURSES CABIN

Location:	Kenai B-3, T3N, R10W, Section 33, Southcentral ½. Near the north shore of Lake Tustumena.
Access:	Powerboat, floatplane, snowmachine, or horse (via the Dr. Pollard Trail).
Construction:	Log construction.
Condition:	Fair condition.
Accommodates:	4-6 persons.
Local Recreation:	Access to Tustumena Lake. Moose hunting.
Hazards:	Strong winds on the lake. Bears.
Firewood:	Available, but not abundant.
Public Use:	25-50 visitors per year.

K32. PIPE CREEK CABIN

Location:	Kenai A-3, T1N, R9W, Section 12, NE ¼; 3½ miles south of Bear Creek off

	Tustumena Lake.
Access:	Primary access to this cabin is by powerboat, floatplane or snowmachine.
Construction:	Dovetail connected logs. The roof is made of spruce poles covered with corrugated metal roofing. The floor is dirt. Four windows provide fair to good lighting.
Condition:	The cabin is in fair condition. However, the spruce poles on the roof are beginning to rot and several base logs show signs of decay.
Accommodates:	2-3 persons.
Local Recreation:	Red salmon spawn in Pipe Creek during late summer. Dolly Varden fishing is possible concurrently. Brown bear hunting during spawning season is also possible in the area.
Hazards:	The shore is exposed to southwesterly winds and breaking waves, which could swamp boats not hauled out on the beach. Bears frequent the area during summer months.
Firewood:	Available, but not abundant.
Public Use:	25-50 visitor days per year.

K33. TRAPPER JOE LAKE CABIN

Location:	Kenai D-1, T8N, R5W, Section 24, SE ¼.
Access:	Primary access to this cabin is by floatplane, snowmachine or four-wheel-drive.
Construction:	Construction is log with a plank floor. The roof is made of spruce poles, covered with corrugated metal roofing. Two windows provide only poor lighting.
Condition:	The cabin is in generally good condition, though several cabin logs have sustained extensive insect damage.
Accommodates:	2-4 persons.
Local Recreation:	Trout fishing in the lake and hunting in the area. Rowboat available at cabin.
Hazards:	Brown and black bears frequent this neck of the woods. Mosquitoes and other insects, though not a severe hazard, are

usually numerous and bothersome because of cabin's close proximity to a marsh.

Firewood: Wood is available, but very limited in supply near the cabin. Some wood can be found along the lakeshore.

Public Use: Receives approximately 200 visitor days per year; 70% summer, 30% winter. 90% of visitors fly in.

K34. VOGEL LAKE

Location: Kenai D-2, TI0N, R7W, Section I, NE ¼.

Access: By floatplane or snowmachine.

Construction: Construction is log with a plywood roof and floor. The roof is covered with asphalt roll roofing. An enclosed porch is attached at the front of the cabin, and the remaining three sides are glassed-in. Lighting is excellent.

Condition: The cabin is generally in good condition although several of the base logs are rotting.

Accommodates: 4-6 persons.

Local Recreation: Fishing and boating are available in Vogel Lake. Hunting is also popular in the area.

Hazards: None.

Firewood: Available, but not abundant.

Public Use: Approximately 100 visitor days per year, primarily during the winter. Cabin has 100% fly-in use.

KENAI FJORDS NATIONAL PARK

Kenai Fjords National Park has four public-use cabins along the coast. They cost $30 per night for parties of up to eight. The maximum stay is three nights. The cabins offer excellent wildlife viewing opportunities and spectacular scenery. They are accessible by floatplane and boat. (Most people use a charter boat.) Once there, a kayak or raft will enhance your opportunity to explore and enjoy the coast. Reservations are required.

Aialik Bay Cabin is on the east side of Aialik Bay and can be located on U.S.G.S. map of Blying Sound D-8; Holgate Arm Cabin is on the west side of Blying Sound (Map D-8); Aialik Bay North Arm Cabin is on the north arm of Nuka Bay (Map Soldovia C-2); Delight Creek Cabin at McCarthy Fjord is on Map Soldovia C-1.

Another cabin is located near Exit Glacier and is only open in the winter with the same restrictions as the other four cabins. Reservations may be made by mail or in person at:

Alaska Public Land Information Center
605 W. 4th Street
Anchorage, AK 99501

ALASKA DIVISION OF PARKS AND OUTDOOR RECREATION

Permits are issued on a first-come, first-served basis. The cabins can be reserved up to six months in advance by paying the required fee. Applicants must be 18 years or older. Conditions are:

- ◆ Clean the cabin after your stay; ensure that the cabin is in same condition as when you arrived.
- ◆ Replace any wood used.
- ◆ Take all trash with you when you leave.
- ◆ Do not leave leftover food.

At Caines Head State Recreation Area, Derby Cove offers a six-man cabin for $35/night. Maximum stay is six nights. For Caines Head State Recreation Area reservations, call the Kenai area office at 907-262-5581.

Kachemak Bay State Park has a cabin at Halibut Cove. It sleeps six people at a cost of $35 per night. Maximum stay is five nights. Call the Homer Ranger Station at 907-235-7024 for reservations.

LOWER SUSITNA UNIT

Kesugi Ridge above Byers Lake.

The lower Susitna Unit encompasses trail opportunities from the Glenn Highway north along the Parks Highway to the northern end of Denali State Park and the Hatcher Pass (Willow-Fishhook) Road. The Susitna River Drainage broadens here, becoming flat and boggy. The trails generally leave the lowlands and stretch into the foothills. Typically, the lower parts of the trails offer little in the way of views. Destinations in the foothills and in the alpine zone give greater distant viewing opportunities. Many of the trail destinations, such as those in Nancy Lakes and Denali State Park, offer unique settings for the hiker/camper, and one can often see Mt. Denali in the distance.

HISTORY

There are many historic trails in the broad valley, but these are generally winter-use ones. Those described here are "pocket" hiking opportunities, as opposed to longer routes. Little use is made of many of these Lower Susitna trails. Thus, if you are looking to get away from other people, these trails may be your *Shangri La*.

THE LAND

The lowlands tend to have more spruce and barren bogs, while the uplands have a mixture of spruce and hardwoods. In the Kesugi Ridge area of Denali State Park, there are pockets of subalpine basins. In the Hatcher Pass area, the vegetation merges into strictly alpine tundra.

WILDLIFE

There are excellent opportunities for viewing moose, the most abundant species. Black bears are plentiful in the area and can be a nuisance.

FYI

You should be aware that most of the trails are minimally maintained. Sometimes washouts and other inconveniences may be encountered.

All trails are coded alpha-numerically starting with LS-1. These codes appear in parentheses next to the name of the trail and on the Lower Susitna Unit regional map.

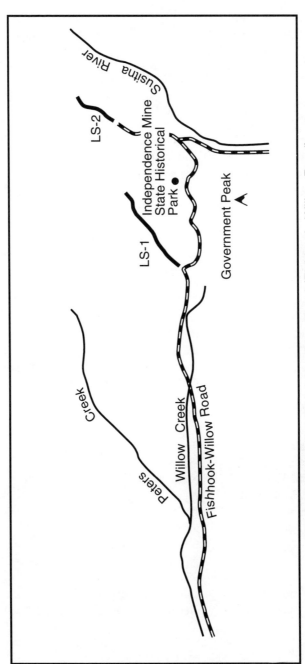

Map showing trails off Hatcher Pass Road (Fishhook–Willow Road)

TRAILS

CRAIGIE CREEK TRAIL (LS-1)

Length (one way):	1.5 miles.
Trip Time (one way):	3 hours.
Degree of Difficulty:	Moderate.
Elevation Gain:	1,000 feet.
Unique Attractions:	Access to the alpine zone.
Area Description:	A beautiful alpine setting at Dogsled Pass. The area is rich in gold mining history. Respect private property as you pass through the area. Schroff Lake is near the terminus of the trail and offers a great backdrop for the photographer.
U.S.G.S. Map:	Anchorage D-7.
Trail Begins:	Take the Hatcher Pass (Fishhook-Willow) Road west of Hatcher Pass; follow left fork in the road. Continue 3.5 miles to Craigie Creek. Turn right just over the creek onto the Craigie Creek Road. Continue for three miles. Park away from the road. The trail is simply an extension of the road. The trip should be made after July 1 so the road will have dried out.
Trail Ends:	At Dogsled Pass.
Condition of Trail:	Fair, unmaintained.
Trail Facilities:	None.
Other Trail Users:	None.
Agency Office:	Alaska State Parks Mat-Su Area Office, HC 32 Box 6706, Wasilla, AK 99654 Phone: (907) 745-3975; FAX: (907) 745-0938.
Season of Use:	Late summer-early fall.
Safety Concerns:	Getting stuck on Craigie Creek.

REED LAKES (LS-2)

Length (one way):	4.5 miles.
Trip Time (one way):	3.5 hours.
Degree of Difficulty:	Moderate to difficult (upper portion).
Elevation Gain:	1,800 feet.
Unique Attractions:	Access to the alpine zone and the lakes.
Area Description:	The lakes are an eyecatching aquamarine color set in the alpine zone, with beautiful rock outcroppings and grassy meadows. The surrounding peaks rise to 6,500 feet and offer some superb views. The lakes do not open until July, so delay your trip until then. The trip is worth it.
U.S.G.S. Map:	Anchorage D-6.
Trail Begins:	Take the Hatcher Pass (Willow-Fishhook) Road out of either Wasilla or Palmer. Drive until it makes a hairpin curve to the left and begins to rise above the Little Susitna River Gorge. Continue one mile from the hairpin and turn a sharp right onto the Fern Mine Road. Drive about 2½ miles and turn right onto a side road to Snowbird Mine (the road runs parallel to Reed Creek). As soon as you turn, find a place to park. Follow that road on foot until it terminates at the Snowbird Mine Buildings. Follow a trail across a foot-bridge over Glacier Creek, near the mouth where it dumps into Reed Creek. Cross Reed Creek on some boulders about 100 yards further. Continue on the trail along the right side of Reed Creek until just below Lower Reed Lake. Cross back to the left side of Reed Creek and go about one mile to Lower Reed Lake. Upper Reed Lake is another mile. Skirt the left side of the falls at the lake.
Trail Ends:	The trail ends just below the falls; you can scramble to the lakes without difficulty.

Condition of Trail:	Fair to just below Lower Reed Lake. Remainder is a route following Reed Creek to Lower and Upper Reed lakes.
Trail Facilities:	There are some undeveloped campsites near upper Reed Lake. There is no firewood.
Other Trail Users:	None.
Agency Contact:	Alaska State Parks Mat-Su Area Office, HC-32 Box 6706, Wasilla, AK 99654 Phone: (907) 745-3975; FAX: (907) 745-0938.
Season of Use:	Late summer/early fall.
Safety Concerns:	Crossing boulders on creek. Possibility of black bears during berry season.

NANCY LAKES CANOE TRAIL SYSTEM (LS-3)

Length (one way):	9-mile loop; Little Su access, 9 miles.
Trip Time (one way):	1-2 days; or 5 hours on the river plus 1 day on a canoe trail.
Degree of Difficulty:	Easy on the loop trail. Short portages. Moderate for Little Su river access.
Unique Attractions:	Canoeing and camping.
Area Description:	Good example of mature glacial lakes and ponds that have productive aquatic ecosystems.
U.S.G.S. Map:	Tyonek C-1.
Trail Begins:	Milepost 4.5 of the Nancy Lake Parkway. The Parkway begins at Milepost 67.3 of the Parks Highway. Or at the Houston access to the Little Su River, Milepost 57.1 of the Parks Highway.
Condition of Trail:	Good.
Trail Facilities:	Public-use cabins (see page 117) and developed portages. Canoe rentals available.
Other Trail Users:	Winter use is primarily snowmobile.
Agency Contact:	Alaska State Parks Mat-Su Area Office, HC 32 Box 6706, Wasilla, AK 99654

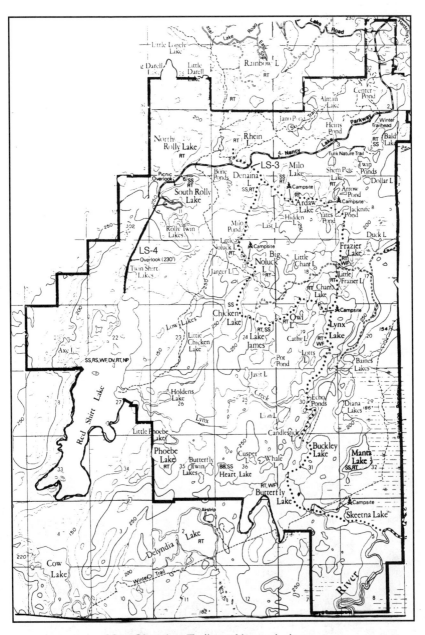

Map Showing Trails at Nancy Lakes
Twin Shirt Lake Trail
Nancy Lakes Canoe Trail • • • •

Phone: (907) 745-3975
Season of Use: Summer.
Safety Concerns: Cold water and hypothermia. Black bears
                            in camp. Overflow in winter. Motor boat
                            wake on river (river channel is narrow).

RED SHIRT LAKE TRAIL (LS-4)

Length (one way):   2.7 miles.
Trip Time (one way):   1.2 hours.
Degree of Difficulty: Easy.
Elevation Gain: Minimal.
Unique Attractions: Access to the lake.
Area Description: Trail follows the forested ridge between
                            the parking lot and Red Shirt Lake.
U.S.G.S. Map: Tyonek C-1.
Trail Begins: End of Nancy Lake Parkway, Milepost 6.5.
Trail Ends: At Red Shirt Lake.
Condition of Trail: Wet in spots.
Trail Facilities: Nine campsites and four public-use cabins
                            (see page 117) at Red Shirt Lake. Canoe
                            rentals available at South Rolly
                            Campground, across from the trailhead.
Other Trail Users: Snowmobilers and cross-country skiers.

Nancy Lakes State Recreation Area.

Agency Contact:	Alaska State Parks, Mat-Su Area Office
	HC-32, Box 6706, Wasilla, AK 99654
	Phone: (907) 745-3975
Season of Use:	Year around.
Safety Concerns:	Cold water and thin ice in early winter.
	Black bear during the summer.

DUTCH CREEK TRAIL (LS-5)

Length (one way):	15 miles.
Trip Time (one way):	10 hours.
Degree of Difficulty:	Moderate to difficult.
Elevation Gain:	1,400 feet.
Unique Attractions:	Views of the Peters Hills, Dutch Hills and Mt. Denali.
Area Description:	The Dutch Hills, rising to 4,700 feet, are a backdrop to the glaciers of Denali National Park. As an extension of the Peters Creek Trail it crosses the Peters Creek Pass into upper Bear Creek and then into Dutch Creek Southcentral Region.
U.S.G.S. Map:	Talkeetna B-3, C-2, C-3.
Trail Begins:	At Bird Creek (See Peters Creek Trail description).
Trail Ends:	Near the mouth of Dutch Creek and the terminus of the Kahiltna Glacier.
Condition of Trail:	Poor, wet in spots.
Trail Facilities:	None.
Other Trail Users:	ATV and snowmachine users.
Agency Contact:	Alaska State Parks
	Mat-Su Area Office, HC-32
	Box 6706
	Wasilla, AK 99654
	(907) 748 3975
Season of Use:	Summer/fall.
Safety Concerns:	Motorized vehicles and extreme weather conditions.

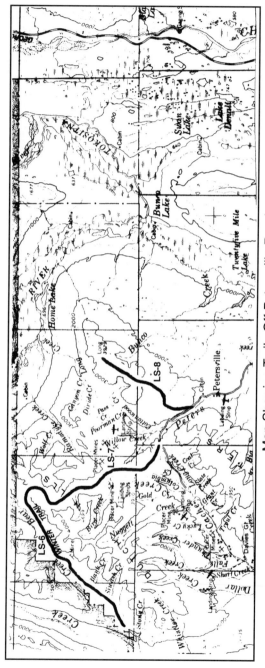

Map Showing Trails Off Petersville Road

Mt. Denali as seen from Denali State Park.

PETERS CREEK TRAIL (LS-6)

Length (one way):	6 miles.
Trip Time (one way):	5 hours.
Degree of Difficulty:	Moderate to difficult.
Elevation Gain:	500 feet.
Unique Attractions:	Access into the Dutch Hills, which rise to 4,700 feet.
Area Description:	Excellent views of the Dutch Hills and historical mining. Opportunities for photography, berry picking and moose hunting. Respect the mining claims and private lands.
U.S.G.S. Map:	Talkeetna C-2.
Trail Begins:	At Milepost 35 of the Petersville Road, about three miles above Petersville. As the road turns southwest and rises out of Peters Creek, the trail starts on the right. The Petersville Road starts at Milepost 114.9 of the Parks Highway (town of Trapper Creek).
Trail Ends:	At Bird Creek junction.
Condition of Trail:	Poor, wet in spots.

Trail Facilities:	None.
Other Trail Users:	Some ATV use on lower trail.
Agency Contact:	Alaska State Parks
	Mat-Su Area Office, HC-32
	Box 6706, Wasilla, AK 99654
	Phone: (907) 745-3975; FAX: (907) 745-0938.
Season of Use:	Summer/fall. Some snowmobiling.
Safety Concerns:	Hypothermia at any time. Black bears; some grizzlies. Steep terrain in upper basin.

LONG POINT TRAIL (LS-7)

Length (one way):	7.5 miles.
Trip Time (one way):	6 hours.
Degree of Difficulty:	Moderate to difficult.
Elevation Gain:	Up to 2,100 feet.
Unique Attractions:	The omnipresence of Mt. Denali and the views of the mountains and Tokositna Valley from the alpine setting. Good berry picking.
Area Description:	The beautiful Peters Hills are accessed via the ATV trail which reaches above the brush line. Follow the ridge north and west another 1½ miles to the first peak (2,840 feet), surrounded by alpine lakes. From there you follow the backbone ridge to the north to Long Peak (3,929 feet). This spot offers a spectacular panorama that really comes alive with the fall colors.
U.S.G.S. Map:	Talkeetna C-2.
Trail Begins:	At Milepost 31 of the Petersville Road. Turn west onto the Petersville Road at Mile 114.9 of the Parks Highway (at the town of Trapper Creek) and travel 19 miles to Forks Roadhouse. Take the right fork here. Travel another 11 miles to the Petersville Placer Mine. The ATV trail angles off to the right about one mile further.

Trail Ends:	The route ends at Long Peak.
Condition of Trail:	Old ATV trail for the first mile, turning into a route above timberline to Long Point.
Trail Facilities:	None.
Other Trail Users:	Possibility of ATV drivers on lower trail.
Agency Contact:	Alaska State Parks
	Mat-Su Area Office, HC 32
	Box 6706, Wasilla, AK 99654
	Phone: (907) 745-3975
Season of Use:	Summer and fall.
Safety Concerns:	Weather conditions and grizzly bears.

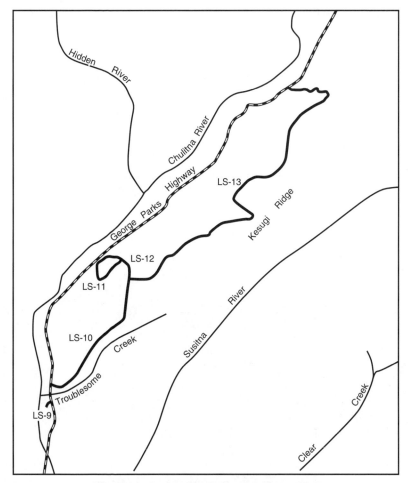

Map showing trails on Denali State Park
(Numbers refer to the succeeding trail descriptions)

CHULITNA CONFLUENCE TRAIL (LS-8)

Length (one way):	1 mile.
Trip Time (one way):	0.5 hours.
Degree of Difficulty:	Easy to moderate.
Elevation Gain:	Minimal.
Unique Attractions:	Viewing salmon spawning and black bear.
U.S.G.S. Map:	Talkeetna C-1.
Area Description:	A salmon-spawning stream, Troublesome Creek, enters directly into the silt-laden Chulitna River.
Trail Begins:	At Milepost 137.5 of the Parks Highway – the Troublesome Creek Campground.
Trail Ends:	Just before the Chulitna River confluence.
Condition of Trail:	Maintained, but wet in spots. Large blowdowns (clusters of trees that have been blown down during a wind storm).
Trail Facilities:	Parking, picnic tables, toilet, well water and bulletin board.
Other Trail Users:	None.
Agency Contact:	Alaska State Parks Mat-Su Area Office, HC 32 Box 6706, Wasilla, AK 99687 Phone: (907) 745-3975; FAX: (907) 745-0938.
Season of Use:	Summer/fall.
Safety Concerns:	Black and grizzly bears; bank erosion undercutting trail.

TROUBLESOME CREEK TRAIL (LS-9)

Length (one way):	12.7 miles; 15.2 miles to Byers Lake Campground.
Trip Time (one way):	8.5 hours; 11 hours to campground.
Degree of Difficulty:	Moderate.
Elevation Gain:	1,500 feet.
Unique Attractions:	Views of Troublesome Creek Basin for the first seven miles.
Area Description:	The trail runs close to Troublesome Creek through the spruce forest then turns north over Kesugi Ridge to the intersection of

Kesugi Ridge and Cascade trails. You can return to Byers Lake Campground via the Cascade Trail or via Kesugi Ridge Trail to the Cold Creek trailhead.

U.S.G.S. Map:	Talkeetna C-1; Talkeetna Mts. C-6.
Trail Begins:	The Upper Troublesome Creek trailhead, about a quarter-mile east of Milepost 137.7 of the Parks Highway.
Trail Ends:	At the Cascade Trail.
Condition of Trail:	Minimal maintenance.
Trail Facilities:	Parking facilities, toilets and signs.
Other Trail Users:	None.
Agency Contact:	Alaska State Parks Mat-Su Area Office, HC 32 Box 6706, Wasilla, AK 99654 Phone: (907) 745-3975 FAX: (907) 745-0938.
Season of Use:	Summer/fall.
Safety Concerns:	Black and grizzly bears.

BYERS LAKE LOOP (LS-10)

Length (one way):	4.8 miles.
Trip Time (one way):	3 hours.
Elevation Gain:	100 feet.
Degree of Difficulty:	Easy.
Unique Attractions:	Access to the entire shoreline of Byers Lake. View spawning red salmon along east shore in late summer.
Area Description:	The trail meanders through large spruce and mixed hardwoods around Byers Lake.
U.S.G.S. Map:	Talkeetna C-1.
Trail Begins:	At Byers Lake Campground.
Condition of Trail:	Maintained.
Trail Facilities:	Parking, hike-in campground on far side of lake, toilet and signs.
Other Trail Users:	Some cross-country skiing.
Agency Contact:	Alaska State Parks Mat-Su Area Office, HC 32 Box 6706, Wasilla, AK 99654 Phone: (907) 745-3975

FAX: (907) 745-0938
Season of Use:	Summer/fall.
Safety Concerns:	Black and grizzly bears.

CASCADE TRAIL (LS-11)

Length (one way):	1.8 miles.
Trip Time (one way):	1.2 hours.
Degree of Difficulty:	Difficult.
Elevation Gain:	1,100 feet.
Unique Attractions:	Access to Kesugi Ridge and Troublesome Creek trails.
Area Description:	Trail passes through spruce forest.
U.S.G.S. Map:	Talkeetna C-1.
Trail Begins:	At the northeast corner of Byers Lake, 1.8 miles up the Byers Lake Loop Trail.
Trail Ends:	At the intersection with Kesugi and Troublesome Creek trails.
Condition of Trail:	Maintained.
Trail Facilities:	Signs.
Other Trail Users:	None.
Agency Contact:	Alaska State Parks Mat-Su Area Office, HC 32 Box 6706, Wasilla, AK 99654 Phone: (907) 745-3975 FAX: (907) 745-0938
Season of Use:	Summer/fall.
Safety Concerns:	Black and grizzly bears.

KESUGI RIDGE TRAIL (LS-12)

Length (one way):	21.5 miles; 25 miles to Byers Lake Campground.
Trip Time (one way):	5 hours; 18 hours to campground.
Degree of Difficulty:	Difficult.
Elevation Gain:	1,500 feet.
Unique Attractions:	Views of the Chulitna Valley.
Area Description:	Leads through spruce/birch forest to alpine tundra.
U.S.G.S. Map:	Talkeetna C-1; Talkeetna Mts. C-6, D-6.

163.9 of the Parks Highway.

Trail Ends:	At the intersection of Troublesome Creek and Cascade Trails.
Condition of Trail:	Maintained.
Trail Facilities:	Parking, toilet, concession stand and signs.
Other Trail Users:	None.
Agency Contact:	Alaska State Parks
	Mat-Su Area Office, HC 32
	Box 6706, Wasilla, AK 99654
	Phone: (907) 745-3975
	FAX: (907) 745-0938
Season of Use:	Summer/fall.
Safety Concerns:	Black and brown bears. Avalanches in winter.

CABINS

Cabins are run by the Alaska Division of Parks and Outdoor Recreation. Permits are issued on a first-come, first-served basis. The cabins sleep from three to 10 people and are equipped with platform beds, a wood stove, benches and a kitchen counter. They may be reserved up to six months in advance by paying the required fee, which varies with each cabin and the size of group. Applicants must be 18 years or older. Canoe rentals are available. Conditions of use are as follows:

♦ Clean the cabin after use, ensuring it is in the same condition as when you arrived.
♦ Replace any wood used.
♦ Take all trash with you when leaving.
♦ Do not leave leftover food/supplies.
♦ Bring sleeping bags and pads, cookstove, firewood and water (or means of purification).

All cabins cost $35 per night.

NANCY LAKE STATE RECREATION AREA CABINS

CABIN	SLEEPS	MAX. STAY
Nancy Lake #1	6	3 nights
Nancy Lake #2	6	3 nights
Nancy Lake #3	6	3 nights
Nancy Lake #4	8	3 nights
Red Shirt Lake #1	7	5 nights
Red Shirt Lake #2	6	5 nights
Red Shirt Lake #3	8	5 nights
Red Shirt Lake #4	8	5 nights
Lynx Lake #1	4	5 nights
Lynx Lake #2	4	5 nights
Lynx Lake #3	4	5 nights
James Lake	6	5 nights

➡ **Note:** Nancy Lake Cabin #1 may be walked or canoed into. Red Shirt Lake Cabin #1 requires both walking and canoeing. Lynx Lake #3 is on the canoe trail system.

DENALI STATE PARK CABINS

CABIN	SLEEPS	MAX STAY
Byers Lake #1	5	3 nights
Byers Lake #2	6	3 nights

Contact:

Alaska State Parks
Mat-Su Area Office
HC 32, Box 6706
Wasilla, AK 99654
Phone: (907) 745-3975
FAX: (907) 745-0938

CHUGACH UNIT

Hiker starting the Eagle River Trail, Chugach State Park.

The Chugach Unit consists of the Chugach Range east to the Lake Louise Road on the Glenn Highway and the southerly drainages of the Talkeetna Mountains on the north side of the Glenn Highway. Included in this unit are some of the public hiking trails within the city of Anchorage. The crown jewel of this unit is Chugach State Park – a 495,000-acre park that rings the greater Anchorage region on the east. It consists of a foothill area offering relatively easy access to the alpine zone. You can see glaciers to the east and Cook Inlet/Turnagain Arm to the west. The historic Iditarod Trail passes through the middle of the park. There is nothing more breathtaking than a view of the Eagle River Canyon on a late summer afternoon, or Crow Glacier accented by the fall alpenglow.

The park receives heavy summer use, concentrated near the trailheads, and motorized vehicles are allowed on some trails (check the individual descriptions).

HISTORY

The other focal point here is the foothill area of the south slope of the Talkeetna Mountains. This is historic mining country dating back to the turn of the century. It offers unique landscapes and regional history. However, the primary use many of these trails has seen is from ATVs, and some routes are not shown on the map. Check with the Parks and Recreation Office of the Mat-Su Borough (Phone: 907-745-9663).

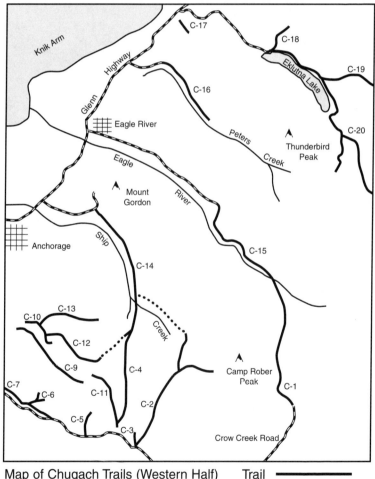

Map of Chugach Trails (Western Half)   Trail ——————
                                        Route •••••••••

➲ While you can enjoy some great moments along these trails, you should be aware that you will be sharing them with motorized users.

You must also remember that the buildings and ruins en route are either private property or protected as a public resource. Please respect those rights.

THE LAND

Most of the trails are not maintained and are subject to flooding and erosion. Many require fording streams, but none should pose a hazard if crossed using proper techniques.

All trails are coded alpha-numerically (C-1, C-2, etc.) and those codes appear in parentheses next to the name of the trail in each trail description and on the Chugach Unit map.

TRAILS

CROW CREEK TRAIL (C-1)

Length (one way):	4.1 miles.
Trip Time (one way):	2.3 hours.
Degree of Difficulty:	Moderate to difficult.
Elevation Gain:	2,000 feet.
Unique Attractions:	Historic Iditarod Trail, historic mining ruins, Raven Glacier and views of the Chugach Mountains and Cook Inlet.
Area Description:	The trail starts in the spruce forest at Milk Creek and quickly ascends through switchbacks to the 3,500-foot elevation, well above timberline. Several glaciers can be seen from Crow Pass, as can spectacular peaks and valleys. Mountain goat and Dall sheep frequent the high country. Because the public-use cabin is

	above timberline, a camp stove is a must
U.S.G.S. Map:	Anchorage A-6, A-7.
Trail Begins:	At the end of the Crow Creek Road. Turn east on the Alyeska Road at Milepost 90 of the Seward Highway. After 1.9 miles the Crow Creek Road turns off to the left. The trailhead is six miles further along a single lane road.
Trail Ends:	At Raven Glacier. The Eagle River Trail (C-15) begins at this point and continues downstream to the Chugach State Park visitor center.
Condition of Trail:	Maintained. Snow persists until mid-June.
Trail Facilities:	Limited parking and trailhead sign. Public-use cabin at Crow Pass (Mile 3). Foot-bridges across creeks.
Other Trail Users:	Open to horse use July through fall season.
Agency Contact:	Glacier Ranger District U.S. Forest Service Girdwood, AK 99587-0129 Phone: (907) 783-3242
Season of Use:	Summer/fall.
Safety Concerns:	Winter and spring use should be avoided due to extreme avalanche conditions.

BIRD CREEK TRAIL (C-2)

Length (one way):	16 miles (first six miles are well developed).
Trip Time (one way):	10 hours.
Degree of Difficulty:	Moderate (steep over Bird Pass).
Elevation Gain:	1,900 feet.
Unique Attractions:	Views of the Chugach Mountains. Distant viewing of Dall sheep.
Area Description:	The trail is located along the creek bottom, with occasional views of Bird Peak to the east and Mount Williwaw to the west. The trail turns up the North Fork of Bird Creek about eight miles in and rises abruptly to Bird Pass (Mile 10). Care

should be taken if continuing on the old trail up the main Bird Creek another three miles, terminating above timberline. After Bird Pass the trail follows the North Fork of Ship Creek downstream to the main stem of Ship Creek.

U.S.G.S. Map:	Anchorage A-7; Seward D-7.
Trail Begins:	About 1.3 miles up a gravel road off Mile 100 of Seward Highway.
Trail Ends:	At Ship Creek.
Condition of Trail:	Developed, but wet in spots. Minimal maintenance over first five miles. Remainder is a primitive trail.
Trail Facilities:	Limited parking and trailhead sign.
Other Trail Users:	Snowmobiles allowed on first six miles of trail. ATVs and mountain bikes are allowed on the old logging roads in Penguin Creek, just before the beginning of the trail.
Agency Contact:	Chugach State Park, HC-52 Box 8999, Indian, AK 99540 Phone: (907) 345-5014 24-hour information: (907) 694-6391
Season of Use:	Summer/fall. Lower Bird Creek also used in winter.
Safety Concerns:	Black bear in the camp during the summer and fall. Avalanche hazard on upper two-thirds of Bird Creek.

BIRD RIDGE TRAIL (C-3)

Length (one way):	2 miles.
Trip Time (one way):	2 hours.
Degree of Difficulty:	Very difficult (steep).
Elevation Gain:	2,000 feet.
Unique Attractions:	Scenic views of Turnagain Arm. Good early displays of alpine wildflowers.
Area Description:	This is a steep, short hike to above timberline for viewing the mountains and Turnagain Arm. Watching the bore tide from the ridge is spectacular. You can

continue on up the ridge for another four miles to overlook Ship Creek. However, there is no trail.

U.S.G.S. Map:	Anchorage A-7; Seward D-7.
Trail Begins:	Just off Mile 102 of the Seward Highway. Turn north into a parking area. The trail-head is marked.
Trail Ends:	At first prominent point on the ridge above timberline.
Condition of Trail:	Good, with foot holds even on steep slopes.
Trail Facilities:	Limited parking and trailhead sign.
Other Trail Users:	None.
Agency Contact:	Chugach State Park, HC-52 Box 8999, Indian, AK 99540 Phone: (907) 345-5014 24-hour information call (907) 694-6391
Season of Use:	Summer/fall.
Safety Concerns:	Steep terrain away from the trail.

INDIAN CREEK PASS TRAIL (C-4)

Length (one way):	6 miles.
Trip Time (one way):	3 hours.
Degree of Difficulty:	Easy to moderate.
Elevation Gain:	2,100 feet.
Unique Attractions:	Periodic views of the mountains. Distant viewing of Dall sheep. Alpine floral displays at the pass. Opportunity for a continuous trip over the pass and down Ship Creek.
Area Description:	The Indian Creek Pass Trail meanders along the east side of the creek, primarily through spruce and spruce-hardwood forests. Periodic views of the mountains are possible. The trail rises above timberline about two miles from the pass, offering panoramic views of the mountains and distant views of Turnagain Arm. Once over the pass into Ship Creek, the trail becomes less distinct until reaching

the North Fork. It actually fords to the east side of the creek a mile before reaching the North Fork. The ford is clearly marked. See Ship Creek Trail for the description from North Fork downstream. There is an interesting side trip about two miles downstream on the fork of Ship Creek that reaches Indian Creek Pass. Turn west upstream on the mainstream of Ship Creek to Ship Lake. This addition is about three miles long.

U.S.G.S. Map:	Anchorage A-7; Seward D-7.
Trail Begins:	About a half-mile up Indian Creek Road turn right and continue another three-quarters of a mile to the trailhead. Indian Creek Road starts at Mile 103 of the Seward Highway.
Trail Ends:	At Indian Creek Pass.
Condition of Trail:	Well defined. Minimal maintenance.
Trail Facilities:	Limited parking and trailhead sign.
Other Trail Users:	Cross-country skiers.
Agency Contact:	Chugach State Park, HC-52 Box 8999, Indian, AK 99540 Phone: (907) 345-5014 24-hour information call (907) 694-6391
Season of Use:	Summer, fall and late winter/early spring (cross-country skiing).
Safety Concerns:	Black bears in camp in summer. Winter storms.

FALLS CREEK TRAIL (C-5)

Length (one way):	1.8 miles.
Trip Time (one way):	1.5 hours.
Degree of Difficulty:	Difficult (moderately steep).
Elevation Gain:	2,200 feet.
Unique Attractions:	Views of Turnagain Arm and alpine zone.
Area Description:	Chugach State Park Trail passes through a mixture of spruce and hardwoods. It is fairly steep in places, leading to the edge of the alpine zone.

U.S.G.S. Map:	Anchorage A-7; Seward D-7.
Trail Begins:	Turn off at Seward Highway Milepost 105.7. Trail follows the ridge on the east side of the creek.
Trail Ends:	Trail terminates at the alpine zone.
Condition of Trail:	Minimal maintenance.
Trail Facilities:	Parking.
Other Trail Users:	None.
Agency Contact:	Chugach State Park, HC-52 Box 8999, Indian, AK 99540 Phone: (907) 345-5014 24-hour information: (907) 694-6391
Season of Use:	Summer/fall.
Safety Concerns:	Avoid during winter due to potential avalanches.

Fireweed in full bloom.

MCHUGH CREEK/TABLE ROCK TRAIL (C-6)

Length (one way):	McHugh Creek, 1 mile; Table Rock, 0.8 miles.
Trip Time (one way):	1 hour (either trip).
Degree of Difficulty:	McHugh Creek - easy to moderate; Table Rock - difficult due to steep terrain.

Elevation Gain:	150 feet (McHugh Creek); 1,000 feet (Table Rock).
Unique Attractions:	Alpine floral displays, views of Turnagain Arm and berry picking.
Area Description:	After turning uphill off the Old Johnson Trail, the trail splits: uphill goes to Table Rock, downhill leads up to McHugh Creek. The uphill climb passes through the alpine zone with spectacular early summer wildflower displays and views of Turnagain Arm. The downhill route leads up McHugh Creek. This route offers good berry picking in season.
U.S.G.S. Map:	Anchorage A-8.
Trail Begins:	Turn off at Mile 111.8 Seward Highway into McHugh Creek State Wayside. Follow the Old Johnson Trail from the lot a short distance to a fork in the trail. Take the right hand trail to where it forks again, uphill to Table Rock, downhill to McHugh Creek.
Trail Ends:	McHugh Creek Trail terminates at the creek where the terrain begins to steepen. Table Rock terminates at Table Rock.
Condition of Trail:	McHugh Creek - minimal maintenance; Table Rock - steep and rocky, slippery when wet.
Trail Facilities:	Excellent parking and signs on Old Johnson Trail.
Other Trail Users:	None.
Agency Contact:	Chugach State Park, HC-52 Box 8999, Indian, AK 99540 Phone: (907) 345-5014 24-hour information: (907) 694-6391
Season of Use:	Summer/early fall.
Safety Concerns:	Steep rocky terrain on the Table Rock Trail. The route up the ridge above Table Rock is very difficult and should be attempted only by experienced mountain hikers. Avoid the area in winter and early spring due to potential avalanches.

OLD JOHNSON TRAIL (C-7)

Length (one way):	1. Potter to McHugh Creek, 3.5 miles; 2. McHugh Creek to Rainbow Valley, 4 miles; 3. Rainbow Valley to Windy Corner, 2.5 miles.
Trip Time (one way):	1. 2 hours; 2. 2.5 hours; 3. 1.5 hours.
Degree of Difficulty:	Easy.
Elevation Gain:	1. 180 feet; 2. 900 feet; 3. 200 feet.
Unique Attractions:	Historic winter trail and scenic views of Turnagain Arm.
Area Description:	The trail parallels the Seward Highway from Milepost 106 to Milepost 115 and can be hiked in three short segments or all at one time. The trail passes spruce/ hardwood forests, reaching prominent overlooks at many points along the way.
U.S.G.S. Map:	Anchorage D-8; Seward D-7.
Trail Begins:	1. Potter trailhead is at Milepost 115 of the Seward Highway. Turn onto the steep road just south of Potter railroad house. The marked trailhead is in the first switchback. 2. McHugh trailhead is a Milepost 112 of the Seward Highway (McHugh Creek Wayside). 3. Rainbo trailhead is at Milepost 108.3 of the Seward Highway. 4. Windy Corner trailhead is at Milepost 106.9.
Trail Ends:	Your hike can begin and end at any one of the above trailheads.
Condition of Trail:	Good.
Trail Facilities:	Parking and access signs.
Other Trail Users:	None (not enough snow for skiing and motorized use not allowed).
Agency Contact:	Chugach State Park, HC-52 Box 8999, Indian, AK 99540 Phone: (907) 345-5014 24-hour information: (907) 694-6391
Season of Use:	All year.
Safety Concerns:	Falling rock along segment 2 (McHugh Creek to Rainbow Valley). No scrambling

on rock outcrops along this segment because they are not stable.

POTTER MARSH INTERPRETIVE TRAIL (C-8)
(Not Shown on Map)

Length (one way):   0.4 miles.
Trip Time (one way):   0.5 hours.
Degree of Difficulty: Easy.
Elevation Gain: Minimal.
Unique Attractions: Opportunity to view waterfowl.
Area Description: This is a small brackish marsh that is designated as Potter Point State Game Refuge. It offers excellent opportunity for viewing waterfowl along the elevated wooden walkway. Take a telephoto lens and get pictures you never thought possible. The walkway is wrapped around the northwest corner of the marsh.
U.S.G.S. Map: Not needed.
Trail Begins: At parking lot off the Seward Highway on the south edge of Anchorage.
Condition of Trail: Excellent.
Trail Facilities: Parking, interpretive signs and raised, wooden boardwalk.
Other Trail Users: None.
Agency Contact: Alaska Department of Fish and Game
                        333 Raspberry Road
                        Anchorage, AK 99518
                        Phone: (907) 344-0541
Season of Use: Primarily spring, summer and early fall.
Safety Concerns: Getting back onto the Seward Highway during high traffic periods.

RABBIT LAKE TRAIL (C-9)

Length (one way):   5.6 miles.
Trip Time (one way):   3 hours.
Degree of Difficulty: Moderate.
Elevation Gain: 1,200 feet.

Unique Attractions: The beautiful alpine basin surrounding Rabbit Lake. Summer alpine floral displays.

Area Description: The access road passes through lower Rabbit Canyon to the mid-canyon area. The trail traverses the north side of the canyon to Rabbit Lake, a picturesque alpine lake. Many mountain peaks and Turnagain Arm can be viewed from the upper part of the trail.

U.S.G.S. Map: Anchorage A-7, A-8.

Trail Begins: Turn east from Seward Highway just south of Anchorage onto DeArmoun Road. Continue across Hillside Drive to upper DeArmoun Road. Turn right onto Lower Canyon Road and continue 1.5 miles to Chugach State Park boundary. The trail begins a half-mile further on.

Trail Ends: At Rabbit Lake.

Condition of Trail: First 3½ miles is rutted from previous ORV use. Last two miles are stable, minimally maintained.

Trail Facilities: Limited parking and signs.

Other Trail Users: Cross-country skiers.

Agency Contact: Chugach State Park, HC-52 Box 8999, Indian, AK 99540 Phone: (907) 345-5014 24-hour information: (907) 694-6391

Season of Use: All year.

Safety Concerns: Winter storms and whiteout conditions.

FLAT TOP MOUNTAIN (C-10)

Length (one way):   2 miles.
Trip Time (one way):   4 hours.
Degree of Difficulty: Moderate to difficult (steep in places).
Elevation Gain: 1,200 feet.
Unique Attractions: Panoramic view from Mt. Denali to Mt. Redoubt.
Area Description: Flat Top Mountain is an easy afternoon climb for a spectacular view of the Alaska

Range and Cook Inlet. This is a trip that even the visitor to Anchorage who has field clothes and well-treaded hiking boots can enjoy.

U.S.G.S. Map:	Anchorage A-8.
Trail Begins:	At the Glen Alps entrance to the Chugach State Park. Take O'Malley Road east from the Seward Highway (about seven miles south from the Glenn Highway). Continue east to Hillside Drive. Turn right on Hillside Drive to Upper Huffman Road. After 0.7 miles on Upper Huffman Road, turn right on Toilsome Hill Drive, then go two miles to the Glen Alps entrance. Take the old four-wheel-drive trail about a quarter-mile and turn right at intersection. Go a short distance then turn right again at the next trail intersection. From here you traverse the slope to the 2,500-foot saddle. A well-defined trail leads up the northwest corner of Flat Top Mountain.
Trail Ends:	At Flat Top Mountain.
Condition of Trail:	Minimal maintenance. Trail is indistinct at upper elevations.
Trail Facilities:	Excellent parking, signs and toilets.
Other Trail Users:	Probably none, except near the entrance.
Agency Contact:	Chugach State Park, HC-52 Box 8999, Indian, AK 99540 Phone: (907) 345-5014 24-hour information: (907)694-6391
Season of Use:	Summer and fall primarily.
Safety Concerns:	Loose rock and steep terrain during summer. Possibility of winter avalanches.

POWERLINE TRAIL (C-11)

Length (one way):	11 miles.
Trip Time (one way):	4.5 hours.
Degree of Difficulty:	Moderate.
Elevation Gain:	1,400 feet.
Unique Attractions:	Easily accessible alpine zone. Views of

	the mountains.
Area Description:	This beautiful high alpine basin above the city of Anchorage offers excellent hiking opportunities and wildflower viewing. It also provides easy access to the Indian Creek Valley.
U.S.G.S. Map:	Anchorage A-7.
Trail Begins:	Trail begins at the Glenn Alps entrance. See the Flat Top Mountain Trail (C-15).
Trail Ends:	At Indian Creek Trail Head, off Mile 102 of the Seward Highway. Note: This is a separate trail from the Indian Creek Trail.
Condition of Trail:	Minimal maintenance. Wet and muddy in early summer.
Trail Facilities:	Excellent parking, toilet facilities and signs.
Other Trail Users:	Snowmobilers in winter on the lower portion of trail.
Agency Contact:	Chugach State Park, HC-52 Box 8999, Indian, AK 99540 Phone: (907) 345-5014 24-hour information: (907) 694-6391
Season of Use:	Primarily summer and fall. Powerline Pass is closed in the winter and the lower portion of the trail is open to snowmobiles.
Safety Concerns:	Hypothermia from chilling storms, particularly early summer or late fall. Avalanches in winter in higher country.

SHIP PASS TRAIL (C-12)

Length (one way):	9 miles.
Trip Time (one way):	5 hours.
Degree of Difficulty:	Moderate.
Elevation Gain:	1,800 feet.
Unique Attractions:	Views of Chugach Mountains and Ship Lake. Access to Ship Creek Trail. Beautiful wildflower displays in mid-summer, as well as fall colors.
Area Description:	The upper South Fork of Campbell Creek is spectacular once you are above the

	brush. Berry picking can be good along the route.
U.S.G.S. Map:	Anchorage A-7, A-8.
Trail Begins:	The trail begins at Glenn Alps entrance. See Flat Top Mountain Trail (C-10) for access description. Follow the Powerline Trail about two miles; then turn left on an old four-wheel-drive trail. Follow it down across the South Fork and then uphill about 0.7 of a mile along the west side of a smaller creek. The developed trail stops where it crosses this smaller creek (out of Hidden Lake). Follow the right hand fork to the east, roughly paralleling the South Fork, until you reach Ship Pass, about 2.5 miles further.
Trail Ends:	The route drops down to Ship Lake and then down further after the fork for about three miles to the main Ship Creek. Turn right, or south, at Ship Creek and it is two miles to Indian Creek Pass. Turn north and go four miles to the junction with North Fork of Ship Creek.
Condition of Trail:	Good, but wet in spots in early summer on lower trail.
Trail Facilities:	Excellent parking, sign at trailhead and comfort station.
Other Trail Users:	Snowmobilers in the winter.
Agency Contact:	Chugach State Park, HC-52 Box 8999, Indian, AK 99540 Phone: (907) 345-5014 24-hour information: (907) 694-6391
Season of Use:	Summer and fall primarily.
Safety Concerns:	Hypothermia during all seasons and whiteouts in the winter.

WILLIWAW TRAIL (C-13)

Length (one way):	7.6 miles.
Trip Time (one way):	4 hours.
Degree of Difficulty:	Moderate to difficult (upper reaches).

Elevation Gain:	1,300 feet.
Unique Attractions:	Easily accessible alpine basin with alpine lakes.
Area Description:	This beautiful alpine valley is star-studded with alpine lakes and provides excellent views of several peaks. Offers overnight camping. Only a short distance from downtown Anchorage. This area provides excellent wildflower viewing and berry picking.
U.S.G.S. Map:	Anchorage A-7, A-8.
Trail Begins:	At the Glen Alps entrance to Chugach State Park. See the Flat Top Mountain Trail (C-10) for access description. Follow the lower trail to the Powerline Trail, turn right for a quarter-mile, then turn downhill on a trail to your left. Cross the South Fork of Campbell Creek and turn left (downstream) on the Middle Fork Loop Trail. After 1½ miles the trail forks. Take the right-hand fork up the Middle Fork of Campbell Creek. The formal trail ends about a third of the way up the mountain. Continue upstream to the lakes.
Trail Ends:	At Williwaw Lakes.
Condition of Trail:	Minimal maintenance; wet in early summer.
Other Trail Users:	Cross-country skiers in winter.
Agency Contact:	Chugach State Park, HC-52 Box 8999, Indian, AK 99540 Phone: (907) 345-5014 24-hour information: (907) 694-6391
Season of Use:	Summer and fall primarily.
Safety Concerns:	The alpine lakes area is an overnight trip. Go prepared. Hypothermia is a concern at any time.

SHIP CREEK TRAIL (C-14)

Length (one way):	9 miles.
Trip Time (one way):	5 hours.

Degree of Difficulty:	Moderate to difficult.
Elevation Gain:	800 feet.
Unique Attractions:	Access to upper Ship Creek. Viewing opportunities for black bear and Dall sheep.
Area Description:	Ship Creek Valley is narrow, providing excellent views of surrounding peaks. Look for black bears near timberline and Dall sheep on the high mountain meadows in the upper valley. Good berry picking during mid- to late summer.
U.S.G.S. Map:	Anchorage A-7.
Trail Begins:	Mile 4 of the Ski Bowl Road, which turns off the Glenn Highway about five miles from the intersection with Seward Highway. The Arctic Valley Ski Area is just another mile further up the road.
Trail Ends:	The developed trail ends at the North Fork. The main trail goes straight and connects over Indian Pass to the Indian Creek trailhead or you can take the right fork two miles before reaching Indian Creek Pass and go to Ship Lake. You can then connect to the Ship Pass Trail. The North Fork of Ship Creek connects through Bird Pass to the Bird Creek trailhead.
Condition of Trail:	Fair to North Fork. Undeveloped trail beyond that point.
Trail Facilities:	Good parking and sign at trailhead.
Other Trail Users:	Cross-country skiers during the winter on lower Ship Creek.
Agency Contact:	Chugach State Park, HC-52 Box 8999, Indian, AK 99540 Phone: (907) 345-5014 24-hour information: (907) 694-6391
Season of Use:	Summer and fall primarily.
Safety Concerns:	Black bear in camp. Avalanche danger in winter, particularly at the passes. Definitely check with Chugach State Park personnel.

EAGLE RIVER (IDITAROD) TRAIL (C-15)

Length (one way):	16.8 miles to Raven Glacier.
Trip Time (one way):	2.1 days.
Degree of Difficulty:	Moderate to difficult.
Elevation Gain:	3,000 feet.
Unique Attractions:	Glacier country in a wilderness setting accessed by a trail. Excellent views of glaciers. Dall sheep and goats above timberline.
Area Description:	Eagle River drainage is a glacial-carved valley that offers excellent opportunity to view glaciers and wildlife. After descending to the valley floor, the trail parallels Eagle River, crossing Icicle Creek (5.5 miles), Twin Falls Creek (8 miles) and Thunder Gorge (10 miles) to Eagle Glacier Lake (11.2 miles). Cairns mark the braided crossing at Icicle Creek. Below the lake a well-marked ford takes the trail across the river at a downstream angle. The trail then turns south and follows Raven Creek, crossing a foot-bridge to the other side about two miles before getting to Raven Glacier. Clean drinking water may be difficult to obtain.
U.S.G.S. Map:	Anchorage A-6, A-7.
Trail Begins:	At the Eagle River Visitor Center. Turn on Eagle River Road (Mile 13, Glenn Highway). Go to end of road.
Trail Ends:	It connects to the Crow Creek Trail at Raven Glacier.
Condition of Trail:	Minimal maintenance. Potential erosion problems.
Trail Facilities:	Parking, visitor center, signs and foot-bridges at Clear and Raven creeks (upper part of the trail).
Other Trail Users:	Horseback riders in late summer.
Agency Contact:	Chugach State Park, HC-52 Box 8999, Indian, AK 99540 Phone: (907) 345-5014

24-hour information: (907) 694-6391

Season of Use: Late summer/fall.
Safety Concerns: Whiteout conditions at any time. Black
                             bears in the camp. Avalanche potential
                             in winter.

PETERS CREEK (C-16)

Length (one way):   6 miles.
Trip Time (one way):   3 hours.
Degree of Difficulty: Moderate.
Elevation Gain: 600 feet.
Unique Attractions: An example of a glacial-carved valley.
                             Good wildlife viewing opportunity –
                             moose, black bear and Dall sheep (above
                             timberline).
Area Description: This is a beautiful, glacial-carved valley that
                             provides stunning vistas of the
                             surrounding mountain peaks and wildlife
                             viewing. The trail terminates about a half-
                             mile before Nine Mile Creek, but it's easy
                             to continue another two miles. The central
                             portion of the trail passes through an
                             easement over private lands.
U.S.G.S. Map: Anchorage B-6, B-7.
Trail Begins: At the end of Peters Creek Road. Turn off
                             at Mile 21 of the Glenn Highway onto
                             Peters Creek Road.
Trail Ends: Just before Nine Mile Creek.
Condition of Trail: Minimal maintenance.
Trail Facilities: Parking and sign.
Other Trail Users: Snowmobilers and cross-country skiers.
Agency Contact: Chugach State Park, HC-52
                             Box 8999, Indian, AK 99540
                             Phone: (907) 345-5014
                             24-hour information: (907) 694-6391
Season of Use: Mostly during summer and fall. Some
                             winter use.
Safety Concerns: Black bear along trail and in camp.
                             Avalanche in winter.

THUNDERBIRD FALLS TRAIL (C-17)

Length (one way):   1 mile.
Trip Time (one way):   0.6 hours.
Degree of Difficulty: Easy to moderate.
Elevation Gain: 200 feet.
Unique Attractions: Thunder Bird Falls.
Area Description: Thunder Bird Falls are hidden in a deeply
                       cut gorge that is rarely penetrated by
                       sunlight. You descend from the parking lot
                       to Thunderbird Creek and then go up-
                       stream about 150 yards to the end of the
                       trail. Do not go beyond this point or climb
                       in the cliffs above the creek.
U.S.G.S. Map: Anchorage B-7.
Trail Begins: At a parking lot next to the Old Glenn
                       Highway. Turn off at Mile 25 of the Glenn
                       Highway, the Thunderbird Falls exit.
                       Watch for the sign.
Trail Ends: At viewing point along the creek.
Condition of Trail: Good. Slick when wet.
Trail Facilities: Parking and signing.
Other Trail Users: None.
Agency Contact: Chugach State Park, HC-52
                       Box 8999, Indian, AK 99540
                       Phone: (907) 345-5014
                       24-hour information: (907) 694-6391
Season of Use: Summer/fall.
Safety Concerns: Steep terrain and swift water. Stay on the
                       trail.

TWIN PEAKS (C-18)

Length (one way):   3 miles.
Trip Time (one way):   2 hours.
Degree of Difficulty: Moderate to difficult.
Elevation Gain: 2,900 feet.
Unique Attractions: A beautiful alpine valley. Viewing
                       opportunities for Dall sheep, black bear
                       and mountain goats. Berry picking in
                       season.

Area Description:	The lower elevations are a mixture of spruce and hardwoods, reaching timberline at 2,700 feet in elevation. The alpine meadow offers good camping, wildlife viewing and wildflower displays.
U.S.G.S. Map:	Anchorage B-6.
Trail Begins:	At the Eklutna Lake Campground. Turn off at Mile 26 of the Glenn Highway onto the Eklutna Road and follow it nine miles to the campground. The access trail begins just across the footbridge from the parking area. Watch for the trail signs.
Trail Ends:	Just above the timberline. Extend this trip by taking the right fork of the creek to the pass at the headwaters. Follow the ridge north to the 5,050-foot knob and then head down to East Twin Peak Pass (4,850 feet). The trail then drops down into the North Fork of the original creek, following it back to the original trail near timberline. This adds about another three miles to the trip.
Condition of Trail:	Minimal maintenance.
Other Trail Users:	None.
Agency Contact:	Chugach State Park, HC-52 Box 8999, Indian, AK 99540 Phone: (907) 345-5014 24-hour information: (907) 694-6391
Season of Use:	Summer/fall.
Safety Concerns:	Black bears and steep terrain.

HUNTER CREEK PASS TRAIL (C-19)

Length (one way):	5.5 miles (11 miles from Eklutna River Campground).
Trip Time (one way):	4.8 hours.
Degree of Difficulty:	Moderate to difficult.
Elevation Gain:	3,400 feet.
Unique Attractions:	Breathtaking views of the Chugach Mountains, outstanding wildlife viewing, excellent berry picking and fall color

displays.

Area Description:
The alpine basin was glacially formed. In fact, the upper reaches contain a large glacial moraine. It manifests all of the good characteristics of a high alpine valley – from wildflowers to berries to wildlife. The trail rises steeply through the spruce-hardwood forest to timberline, about 2,500 feet elevation.

U.S.G.S. Map:
Anchorage B-6.

Trail Begins:
At the Eklutna Campground (turn off at Mile 26 of the Glenn Highway and go nine miles).

Trail Ends:
At Hunter Pass. You are on your own after that.

Condition of Trail:
Minimal maintenance during the first mile or so.

Trail Facilities:
Parking and signs.

Other Trail Users:
Those driving ATVs and bikers on the portion around Eklutna Lake.

Agency Contact:
Chugach State Park, HC-52 Box 8999, Indian, AK 99540 Phone: (907) 345-5014 24-hour information call (907)694-6391

Season of Use:
Summer/fall.

Safety Concerns:
Steep, rocky terrain in the high country. Winter avalanche conditions. Black bears in the camp.

EAST FORK (C-20)

Length (one way):
14 miles.

Trip Time (one way):
4.5 hours.

Degree of Difficulty:
Easy to moderate.

Elevation Gain:
1,300 feet.

Unique Attractions:
Access to the glacial country in the upper reaches of the Eklutna River. Excellent wildlife viewing for Dall sheep, mountain goats and black bear.

Area Description:
Most of the trail is along the east side of

Eklutna Lake. It then turns up the East Fork of the Eklutna River. The valley becomes narrow and glaciers hang on the high peaks (8,000 feet). It is the home of sheep and goats, wolves, pika, ground squirrels, and more – plus some terrible weather coming off the glaciers.

U.S.G.S. Map:	Anchorage B-6.
Trail Begins:	At the Eklutna River Campground.
Trail Ends:	About three miles from the foot of the East Fork Glacier.
Condition of Trail:	First 10 miles is an old road; next three miles up the East Fork are minimally maintained; and the last 1.5 miles, an undesignated trail above timberline.
Trail Facilities:	Parking and signs. Developed campsites near confluence of the East Fork and the main Eklutna.
Other Trail Users:	ATVs can use the road along the lake on Wednesday through Saturday. Snow-mobilers are allowed in the same location.
Agency Contact:	Chugach State Park, HC-52 Box 8999, Indian, AK 99540 Phone: (907) 345-5014 24-hour information: (907) 694-6391
Season of Use:	Summer/fall.
Safety Concerns:	Whiteouts and hypothermia. Black bear in the camp. Deep, swift glacial waters. Avoid the East Fork drainage in winter because of avalanche danger.

TONY KNOWLES COASTAL TRAIL (C-21)

Length (one way):	9 miles.
Unique Attractions:	View Knik Arm. Exercise trail.
Trail Begins and Ends:	Near the west end of 4th Avenue and Kincaid Park.

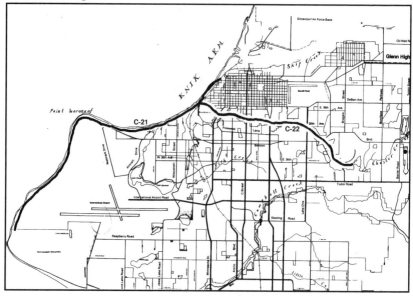

Anchorage Trails Available to the Downtown Visitor

CHESTER CREEK TRAIL SYSTEM (C-22)

Length (one way):	6 miles.
Unique Attractions:	Greenbelt within the urban area and Lagoon Nature Trail segment.
Trail Begins and Ends:	At Westchester Lagoon and University of Alaska, Anchorage.

BAXTER BOG NATURE TRAIL (C-23)

Length (one way):	0.4 miles.
Unique Attractions:	Baxter Bog.
Trail Begins:	Just off Baxter Road. Take Tudor Road east to Baxter Road.
Trail Facilities:	Parking signs and hard trail.
Agency Contact:	Anchorage Parks and Recreation Phone: (907) 343-4474
Safety Concerns:	Watch for bikers.

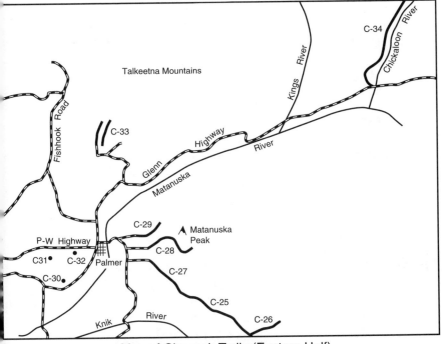

Map of Chugach Trails (Eastern Half)

KNIK GLACIER TRAIL (C-25)

Length (one way):	20 miles.
Trip Time (one way):	10 hours.
Degree of Difficulty:	Moderate.
Elevation Gain: 200 feet.	
Unique Attractions:	View of Knik Glacier. Access to the middle portion of the Knik River Valley.
Area Description:	Trail parallels the north side of the Knik River terminating on the braided river bottom across from Knik Glacier and just before the Glacier Fork of the Knik River. You have to ford Jim Creek, Friday Creek and river braids on the middle part of the river. This is really exciting wild country with moose and bear near the river and mountain goat and Dall sheep on the upper slopes.
U.S.G.S. Map:	Anchorage B-5, C-5, C-6.

Trail Begins:	About 2.5 miles from the end of Caudill Road. Turn off at Mile 11.5 of the Old Glenn Highway onto Plumley Road. Go 1.4 miles and turn right on Caudill Road. Go about 0.8 miles to the Jim Creek Road turnoff. Turn left on a primitive road for 1.8 miles.
Trail Ends:	About one mile before reaching the Glacier Fork of the Knik River.
Condition of Trail:	Wet and not maintained. Because of flooding, some portions of the old trail may be impassable. Detours become necessary.
Trail Facilities:	None.
Other Trail Users:	Snowmobilers in winter. Some ATVs, trail bikes and horses in fall.
Agency Contact:	Matanuska-Susitna Borough Parks and Recreation Division 350 E. Dahlia Ave. Palmer, AK 99645 Phone: (907) 745-9636
Season of Use:	All year, except in the spring.
Safety Concerns:	Cold, swift glacier waters to be crossed. Black or brown bear in the camp. Whiteouts on the upper half of trail. Trail becomes difficult to follow. Avoid water crossings where the water is swift and the bottom difficult to read.

OSWALD TRAIL (C-26)

Length (one way):	3 miles.
Trip Time (one way):	1.8 hours.
Degree of Difficulty:	Difficult.
Elevation Gain:	1,400 feet.
Unique Attractions:	Access to alpine zone from Knik Glacier Trail.
Area Description:	The trail is an access to an old mine developed by Joe Oswald. Mountain goats and sheep inhabit the ridges above the mine. There are spectacular views of

	the Knik River Valley and the peaks on the south side of the river.
U.S.G.S. Map:	Anchorage B-5, C-5.
Trail Begins:	On west side of Friday Creek, intercepting the Knik Glacier Trail.
Trail Ends:	Above timberline at the 2,500-foot level.
Condition of Trail:	Poor. Unmaintained.
Trail Facilities:	None.
Other Trail Users:	None.
Agency Contact:	Matanuska-Susitna Borough Parks and Recreation Division 350 E. Dahlia Ave. Palmer, AK 99645 Phone: (907) 745-9636
Season of Use:	Summer/fall.
Safety Concerns:	Black bears in the camp.

RIPPY TRAIL (C-27)

Length (one way):	5.5 miles.
Trip Time (one way):	2.5 hours.
Degree of Difficulty:	Moderate.
Elevation Gain:	Minimal.
Unique Attractions:	Access to Jim Lake (fishing for Dolly Varden trout and silver salmon (land-locked) and the beginning of the Knik Glacier Trail.
Area Description:	The trail is a good gravel trail to Jim Lake below Matanuska Peak. The fishing in Jim Lake is fair.
U.S.G.S. Map:	Anchorage C-6.
Trail Begins:	At the end of Maud Road. Turn off at Mile 14.6 of the Old Glenn Highway onto Maud Road.
Trail Ends:	Where the trail divides into three forks at Jim Lake. Take the right fork for the continuation as Knik Glacier Trail. It is a very primitive trail to Friday Creek.
Condition of Trail:	Poor. Wet.
Trail Facilities:	None.
Other Trail Users:	Snowmobilers, ORV and trail bike users.

Agency Contact:	Matanuska-Susitna Borough Parks and Recreation Division 350 E. Dahlia Ave. Palmer, AK 99645 Phone: (907) 745-9636
Season of Use:	Summer/fall.
Safety Concerns:	Black bear in camp.

MANTANUSKA PEAK TRAIL (C-28)

Length (one way):	9.5 miles (6.5 miles of trail).
Trip Time (one way):	5.8 hours (3.5 hours).
Degree of Difficulty:	Moderate to difficult.
Elevation Gain:	5,500 feet.
Unique Attractions:	Scrambling to Matanuska Peak and the panoramic views of the valley and the Chugach Mountains. Possibility of seeing sheep and goats up close.
Area Description:	All but the first couple of miles are in the McRoberts Creek drainage. It is a narrow valley of birch and cottonwood, with scattered wet openings of grass and alder. Above timberline is typical subalpine with good wildflower displays and the beginnings of sheep and goat habitat. Look for sheep in the steep mountain slopes east of Matanuska Peak.
U.S.G.S. Map:	Anchorage C-5, C-6.
Trail Begins:	At the end of Smith Road. Turn onto Smith Road at Mile 15.6 of the Old Glenn Highway and continue 1.4 miles until the junction with Harmony Avenue. Park off the road.
Trail Ends:	In the upper reaches of McRoberts Creek. It is a direct route up to the ridge to Matanuska Peak. From a deep gully above treeline to the summit of Matanuska Peak is marked with fiberglass and wood stakes.
Condition of Trail:	Minimal maintenance. Wet in spots.
Trail Facilities:	None.

Other Trail Users:	Horseback riders to the upper valley trail.
Agency Contact:	Matanuska-Susitna Borough
	Parks and Recreation Division
	350 E. Dahlia Ave.
	Palmer, AK 99645
	Phone: (907) 745-9636
Season of Use:	Summer/fall. Occasional winter use.
Safety Concerns:	Black bears in the camp. Steep, rocky terrain near Matanuska Peak. Whiteouts and hypothermia above timberline.

LAZY MOUNTAIN (C-29)

Length (one way):	2.5 miles.
Trip Time (one way):	4 hours.
Degree of Difficulty:	Difficult to the main ridge, then easy to the summit.
Elevation Gain:	3,100 feet.
Unique Attractions:	Views of the Matanuska Valley and wildflower displays.
Area Description:	This trail offers outstanding views of the Matanuska Valley and the Talkeetna Mountains. The midsummer wildflower displays are exceptional.
U.S.G.S. Map:	Anchorage C-6.
Trail Begins:	Turn off Mile 16.2 of the Old Glenn Highway onto the Clark-Wolverine Road. Go 0.6 miles to a "T." Turn right and travel one mile until you reach a fork in the road. Take the right fork 0.2 miles to a parking lot.
Trail Ends:	At Lazy Mountain. Those who are skilled at scrambling can take the ridgeline another 4½ miles to Matanuska Peak.
Condition of Trail:	Minimal maintenance. First section of trail is occasionally wet and muddy. Upper section is steep with difficult footing.
Trail Facilities:	Parking.
Other Trail Users:	None.
Agency Contact:	Matanuska-Susitna Borough
	Parks and Recreation Division

350 E. Dahlia Ave.
Palmer, AK 99645
Phone: (907) 745-9636

Season of Use:	Summer/fall.
Safety Concerns:	Steep terrain.

KEPLER-BRADLEY LAKES (C-30)

Length (one way):	3-4 miles of trail segments.
Trip Time (one way):	Varies.
Degree of Difficulty:	Easy.
Elevation Gain:	Minimal.
Unique Attractions:	Easy hiking and good fishing for rainbow trout.
Area Description:	The area offers easy hiking in a rolling, rural landscape. There's good lake fishing for rainbow trout, silver salmon (land-locked) and grayling. This is a good family outing for picnicking, hiking and fishing. There are some private lands that are marked.
U.S.G.S. Map:	C-6.
Trail Begins:	At the end of the access roads off Mile 36.4 and Mile 38 of the Glenn Highway.
Trail Ends:	At the two parking areas and at the various lakes.
Condition of Trail:	Minimal maintenance.
Trail Facilities:	Parking, signs and picnic facilities.
Other Trail Users:	Horseback riders from Matanuska Guest Ranch and Riding Stable.
Agency Contact:	Alaska State Parks Mat-Su Area Office, HC 32 Box 6706, Wasilla, AK 99654 Phone: (907) 745-3975 FAX: (907) 745-0938
Season of Use:	Summer/fall, with some ice fishing in the winter.
Safety Concerns:	Deep cold water of the lakes in the summer and thin ice in the early winter.

MAT-SU COLLEGE NATURE TRAIL (C-31)

Length (one way):	1.5 miles.
Trip Time (one way):	1 hour.
Degree of Difficulty:	Easy.
Elevation Gain:	Minimal.
Unique Attractions:	Native plants and soil pits.
Area Description:	The trail winds its way across old moraine deposits, emphasizing native vegetation and soil development after glaciation. A brochure is available at the college.
U.S.G.S. Map:	Not necessary.
Trail Begins and Ends:	At the Mat-Su Community College. Turn off Glenn Highway at Mile 35.5 onto Parks Highway. Within a half-mile turn right on the Trunk Road. Go 1.8 miles and watch for the college entrance sign on the right.
Condition of Trail:	Minimal maintenance.
Trail Facilities:	Parking, soil pits, signs and benches for resting.
Other Trail Users:	Some cross-country skiers in the winter.
Agency Contact:	Mat-Su College Box 2889 Palmer, AK 99645
Season of Use:	Summer/fall.
Safety Concerns:	Minimal.

CREVASSE MORAINE TRAIL (C-32)

Length:	Thirteen loops totalling 6.7 miles.
Trip Time:	Varies.
Degree of Difficulty:	Easy.
Elevation Gain:	150 feet.
Unique Attractions:	Hiking and running opportunities, as well as birdwatching.
Area Description:	The area is heavily wooded with white birch and white spruce. Some distant views are available from the ridges. The topography is glacially formed. The ridges, called kames, were formed by the

accumulation of debris in major crevasses and the wet depressions, kettles, were formed by melting ice masses.

U.S.G.S. Map:	Not necessary.
Trail Begins and Ends:	At the end of Loma Prieta Drive. Turn south on Loma Prieta Drive at Mile 2.1 of the Palmer-Wasilla Highway.
Condition of Trail:	Moderately well maintained.
Trail Facilities:	Parking area. Sign and fiberglass markers at trail junctions.
Other Trail Users:	Cross-country skiing in the winter.
Agency Contact:	Mat-Su Borough Parks and Recreation Division 350 E. Dahlia Ave. Palmer, AK 99645 Phone: (907) 745-9636
Season of Use:	All year.
Safety Concerns:	Minimal.

SKYLINE TRAILS (C-33)

Length (one way):	1 mile (each trail).
Trip Time (one way):	0.7 hours.
Degree of Difficulty:	Moderate.
Elevation Gain:	600 feet (each trail).
Unique Attractions:	Access to the subalpine zone of the southern edge of the Talkeetna Mountains.
Area Description:	The trails are about three-quarters of a mile apart and terminate in the foothill of Arkose Ridge. There are good wildflower displays and good moose viewing from the foothill. A few ptarmigan can be found on the slopes of Arkose Ridge.
U.S.G.S. Map:	Anchorage C-6, D-6.
Trail Begins:	Both trails begin off the Murphy Road extension. Turn onto Buffalo Mine Road at Mile 53.1 of the Glenn Highway. Travel about three miles to Murphy Road and turn left.
Trail Ends:	At the subalpine tundra.

Condition of Trail:	Poor.
Trail Facilities:	None.
Other Trail Users:	Some cross-country skiers in the winter.
Agency Contact:	Matanuska-Susitna Borough
	Parks and Recreation Division
	350 E. Dahlia Ave.
	Palmer, AK 99645
	Phone: (907) 745-9636
Season of Use:	Summer/fall.
Safety Concerns:	Minimal.

CHICKALOON RIVER (C-34)

Length (one way):	28 miles.
Trip Time (one way):	2.2 days (hiking).
Degree of Difficulty:	Very difficult.
Elevation Gain:	2,900 feet.
Unique Attractions:	Access to the Talkeetna Mountains and the Talkeetna River Pass.
Area Description:	This is an historic mining trail between the towns of Chickaloon and Talkeetna. The original route went from the Talkeetna River Pass (the termination point of this trail) down the river to Yellow Jacket Creek, up Yellow Jacket Creek over a pass and into Iron Creek. It then headed down Iron Creek to Rainbow Lake Pass and into Sheep River to Talkeetna. Much of it is eroded or grown over. It is NOT a recommended route.
U.S.G.S. Map:	Anchorage D-4, Talkeetna Mountains B-3.
Trail Begins:	Turn off at Mile 77 of the Glenn Highway and go as far as you can. Take off from there.
Trail Ends:	At the Talkeetna River Pass (or Camel's Back Pass).
Condition of Trail:	Wet. Washed out in places.
Trail Facilities:	None.
Other Trail Users:	ATV drivers.
Agency Contact:	Matanuska-Susitna Borough
	Parks and Recreation Division

350 E. Dahlia Ave.
Palmer, AK 99645
Phone: (907) 745-9636
Season of Use: Late summer and early fall.
Safety Concerns: Cold, swift water of the river. Bears in the
                        camp. Exhaustion and hypothermia. Be
                        prepared for any medical emergency as
                        you will be a long way from help.

CABINS

CHUGACH FOREST SERVICE

C1. Crow Pass – An A-frame cabin with loft on Crow Creek Trail (Mile 3). Bunks six (sleeps 10). No stove. No firewood. Cabin above timberline. Main attractions are the alpine setting, mining ruins and large glacier.

Wildlife viewing includes black and brown bears, goats and moose. Available June 1 - September 30 only. Closed in winter and spring because of high avalanche danger. Elevation 3,400 feet.

*An A-Frame public-use cabin,
Chugach National Forest.*

KODIAK UNIT

Barometer Mountain on Kodiak Island.

GEOGRAPHY

Kodiak is an island that lies about 100 miles south-southwest of the port of Homer. It is home to the giant Kodiak brown bear, Sitka blacktail deer (introduced) and excellent salmon/steelhead fishing. The island is 100 miles long and 50 miles wide, with nearly two-thirds of the area in the Kodiak National Wildlife Refuge. It is part of the Greater Kodiak Archipelago.

PLANT LIFE

The island supports a variety of plant life from Sitka spruce to alpine flowers. The Sitka spruce occurs at the lower elevation on the northern part of the island. Much of the remainder of the island is dominated by "man-eating" alder stands – often so thick and low to the ground they frustrate even the serious hiker. Once you arrive at treeline, the alpine environment is heaven – spectacular vistas, wildflower displays and less-impeded travel. Often wildflowers bloom in May at lower elevations before everything "greens" up. Some of the wildflowers found here are unique to the archipelago and further west to the Aleutian Islands. Bring your identification book.

In July, August and September the wild berries ripen – blueberries, salmonberries and low- and high-bush cranberries. On a recent fishing trip along the Kodiak road system, I picked about two gallons of cranberries in an hour!

The intertidal zones (exposed during low tides) offer some unique opportunities to view the little critters of the sea – barnacles, mussels, starfish, anemones, limpets, an array of clams (careful of paralytic shellfish poisoning), a variety of small fishes and a few other surprises. The color patterns of the intertidal zones are a must-see even for the casual hiker.

WILDLIFE

Marine mammals are also abundant, from whales to the furry denizens. Sea otters, Steller sea lions and harbor seals can often be viewed from shore. In fact, the seals and sea lions often haul themselves out onto the rocky shoreline for an afternoon siesta. The sea otters usually hang around the kelp beds and may be seen resting on their backs while breaking open a clam shell on their tummies.

There is a tremendous variety of birds, particularly marine birds, such as Steller's eider, oldsquaw and harlequin ducks, and tufted puffins. In fact, many birdwatchers travel to Kodiak in search of the more unusual birds, such as red-throated loon, emperor goose, king eider and Aleutian tern. The Kodiak National Wildlife Refuge publishes a bird checklist indicating the species, seasons and relative abundance.

Large mammals include the Kodiak brown bear, Sitka blacktail deer and foxes, colored from red to silver to black. The brown bears are scattered throughout the island, although their population is less dense near the road system. The typical hiker along the road system would rarely see any tracks, much less see a bear. But you still have to be mentally prepared for such an event.

Given the opportunity, a bear will flee upon seeing humans. When defending their young or their evening meal, they can be aggressive. Do not panic. Talk in a soft voice and back away. Do not run. Most charges are bluffs. For more information, refer to page 23 or contact:

Kodiak National Wildlife Refuge
P.O. Box 825
Kodiak, AK 99615
(907) 487-2600

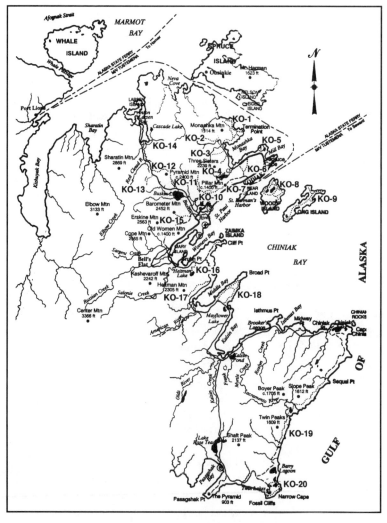

Kodiak Island Road System Trails

Sitka blacktail deer are prevalent throughout the island; however, a series of bad winters have reduced their numbers considerably on the northern half. It is a small deer with big ears and with a rather furtive life style.

Probably most people associate Kodiak with salmon. All four species of salmon occur in Kodiak's streams, along with a local population of Dolly Varden, arctic grayling, char and rainbow trout. Steelhead are found in a few streams on the southwest part of the island. Those streams near the road system hold primarily red and silver salmon and Dolly Varden trout.

Why is all this so important to the hiker if this isolated island has a minimal road system and nearly impenetrable alder thickets? First, Kodiak is accessible via the marine highway system from Homer (and you can bring your vehicle) and scheduled daily airline flights and auto rentals. Yes, the road system is limited, but you can get to some exciting landscapes and excellent hiking opportunities on trails with minimum probability of encountering Mr. Bruin. If you are already planning a trip to Kodiak, extend it a few days and enjoy some of the coastline, alpine mountain peaks and coastal vistas – most within easy driving from the city of Kodiak. Most are day trips; some are overnight.

TRAILS

TERMINATION POINT (KO-1)

Length (one way):	3.5-5 miles.
Trip Time (one way):	2.5-3.5 hours.
Degree of Difficulty:	Easy to moderate.
Elevation Gain:	150 feet.
Unique Attractions:	Views of the coastline. Virgin Sitka spruce forest.
Area Description:	Most of the hiking is through a large stand of virgin Sitka spruce. Thus, the viewing is close-in, except coastal areas such as Termination Point. Free permit required. (Or you may obtain a permit in Kodiak at Buskin River Inn, Westmark Hotel, Mack's Sport Shop, or Cy's Sporting Goods.

U.S.G.S. Map:	Kodiak D-2.
Trail Begins:	At the end of the Monashka Bay Road.
Trail Ends:	About 1½ miles west of Azimuth Point.
Condition of Trail:	No maintenance. Wet in spots.
Trail Facilities:	None.
Other Trail Users:	None.
Agency Contact:	Leisnoi Village Corporation
	424 Marine Way, Kodiak, AK 99615
	Phone: (907) 487-8191
Season of Use:	Spring/summer/fall.
Safety Concerns:	Hypothermia and abrupt change in weather conditions.

MONASHKA CREEK (KO-2)

Length (one way):	2.1 miles.
Trip Time (one way):	1.2 hours.
Degree of Difficulty:	Moderate.
Elevation Gain:	800 feet.
Unique Attractions:	Access to Monashka Creek Reservoir and the ridge to the north.
Area Description:	The trail follows the road to the reservoir, crosses Monashka Creek and then heads up the ridge to the high point northwest of Monashka Reservoir.
U.S.G.S. Map:	Kodiak D-2.
Trail Begins:	Near the mouth of Monashka Creek.
Trail Ends:	At the reservoir.
Condition of Trail:	Access road to city water reservoir, but unmaintained beyond that point.
Trail Facilities:	Minimal parking.
Other Trail Users:	None.
Agency Contact:	Resource Management Officer
	Kodiak Island Borough
	710 Mill Bay Road
	Kodiak, AK 99615
	Phone: (907) 486-5736
Season of Use:	All seasons.
Safety Concerns:	Hypothermia.

DEVILS PRONGS TRAIL (KO-3)

Length (one way):	1.8 miles.
Trip Time (one way):	0.8 hours.
Degree of Difficulty:	Moderate to difficult.
Elevation Gain:	1,700 feet.
Unique Attractions:	Access to the low mountains, called the Devils Prongs. View of Monashka Bay.
Area Description:	The trail goes through dense brush and alders to high country at the Devils Prongs. There are good views of Monashka Bay.
U.S.G.S. Map:	Kodiak D-2.
Trail Begins:	About midway along the head of Monashka Bay along the Pillar Creek Road. Look for an old four-wheel road on left, about 6.2 miles from Ft. Abercrombie State Park.
Trail Ends:	Near Devils Prongs (elevation 2,097 feet).
Condition of Trail:	Unmaintained.
Trail Facilities:	Minimal parking.
Other Trail Users:	None.
Agency Contact:	Resource Management Officer Kodiak Island Borough 710 Mill Bay Road, Kodiak, AK 99615 Phone: (907) 486-5736
Season of Use:	Summer/fall.
Safety Concerns:	Hypothermia.

DEVILS PRONGS SOUTH (KO-4)

Length (one way):	1.7 miles (into the foothills).
Trip Time (one way):	1.2 hours.
Degree of Difficulty:	Moderate, unless you venture to the top of one of the Prongs.
Elevation Gain:	350 feet.
Unique Attractions:	Hiking in the foothills of the Devils Prongs. Several routes to the top of the Prongs.
Area Description:	This is brush country, but you have an excellent view of the alpine country. The trail itself is an old four-wheel drive route.
U.S.G.S. Map:	Kodiak D-2.

Trail Begins:	On Monashka Bay Road, 4.9 miles from Fort Abercrombie State Park.
Trail Ends:	In the foothills below the most westerly of the Devils Prongs.
Condition of Trail:	Unmaintained.
Trail Facilities:	Minimal parking.
Other Trail Users:	Possibly some four-wheelers.
Agency Contact:	Resource Management Officer Kodiak Island Borough 710 Mill Bay Road Kodiak, AK 99615 Phone: (907) 486-5736
Season of Use:	Primarily summer and fall.
Safety Concerns:	Minimal.

FORT ABERCROMBIE STATE PARK (KO-5)

Length (one way):	Varies.
Trip Time (one way):	Varies.
Degree of Difficulty:	Some trails are easy; others more difficult.
Elevation Gain:	Minimal.
Unique Attractions:	The old fort, views of the rugged coastline and fishing in Abercombie Lake for grayling and rainbow trout.
Area Description:	This is a ruggedly beautiful coastal area, called Miller Point. It was built to protect the Kodiak Naval Base and the town of Kodiak during WWII.
U.S.G.S. Map:	Kodiak D-2.
Trail Begins:	Several locations. Trails are generally short and well-marked.
Condition of Trail:	Minimal maintenance.
Trail Facilities:	Parking, signs and a trail map (at the Headquarters visitor center).
Other Trail Users:	None.
Agency Contact:	Alaska State Parks, Kodiak District SR Box 3800, Kodiak, AK 99615 Phone: (907) 486-6339
Season of Use:	Summer/fall.
Safety Concerns:	Some cliffs near the trail/roads. Sheer drop-offs into the ocean.

LOWER RESERVOIR TRAIL (KO-6)

Length (one way):	1.2 miles.
Trip Time (one way):	0.7 hours.
Degree of Difficulty:	Easy.
Elevation Gain:	80 feet.
Unique Attractions:	Good, easy family hiking opportunity.
Area Description:	This is a good route to the Lower Reservoir. It then loops around the southern end of Lower Reservoir on a four-wheel-drive trail to Manashka Bay Road (about 2.4 miles from Abercrombie State Park).
U.S.G.S. Map:	Kodiak D-2.
Trail Begins:	At Mile 0.2 take the Pillar Mountain Road (a gated road to the right). Turn left on Thorsheim (at MacDonalds), go to Maple Avenue and turn left again. Maple Avenue turns into Pillar Mountain Road.
Trail Ends:	At Monashka Bay Road.
Condition of Trail:	Unmaintained four-wheel drive trail.
Trail Facilities:	None.
Other Trail Users:	None.
Agency Contact:	Resource Management Officer Kodiak Island Borough 710 Mill Bay Road Kodiak, AK 99615 Phone: (907) 486-5736
Season of Use:	Summer/fall.
Safety Concerns:	Minimal.

NEAR ISLAND (KO-7)

Length (one way):	Varies.
Trip Time (one way):	Varies.
Degree of Difficulty:	Easy to moderate.
Elevation Gain:	Minimal.
Unique Attractions:	Eagle viewing and free-ranging ponies. Views of bays and the intertidal zone.
Area Description:	The island is connected to downtown Kodiak via a modern bridge. A good trail

for the north end of Kodiak begins just after the bridge. Look for a sign on the left. Work is underway to extend this around the entire perimeter of the island. There is an excellent tidal pool on the northeast corner of the island.

U.S.G.S. Map:	Kodiak D-2.
Trail Begins:	Just over the bridge.
Trail Ends:	Loops back to the beginning.
Condition of Trail:	Minimal maintenance. Wet in spots.
Trail Facilities:	Minimal parking and signs. Some benches and picnic tables.
Other Trail Users:	Some domestic ponies and cows.
Agency Contact:	Resource Management Officer Kodiak Island Borough 710 Mill Bay Road Kodiak, AK 99615 Phone: (907) 486-5736
Season of Use:	Spring through fall.
Safety Concerns:	Be careful of uneven trail sections.

WOODY ISLAND (KO-8)

Length (one way):	Varies.
Trip Time (one way):	Varies.
Degree of Difficulty:	Easy.
Elevation Gain:	Minimal.
Unique Attractions:	Island vegetation and an old Russian cemetery.
Area Description:	There is a mixture of land ownership on the island – private, Kodiak Borough and State of Alaska. Check with Kodiak Borough before going.
U.S.G.S. Map:	Kodiak D-2.
Trail Begins:	At several locations on northern end of the island.
Condition of Trail:	Not maintained.
Trail Facilities:	None.
Other Trail Users:	None.
Agency Contact:	Resource Management Officer Kodiak Island Borough

710 Mill Bay Road
Kodiak, AK 99615
Phone: (907) 486-5736

Season of Use:	Summer/fall.
Safety Concerns:	Minimal. Watch weather patterns.

LONG ISLAND (KO-9)

Length (one way):	Varies from one to several miles.
Trip Time (one way):	Varies.
Degree of Difficulty:	Easy.
Elevation Gain:	Minimal.
Unique Attractions:	Island vegetation and World War II emplacements. Exploring.
Area Description:	The area has a maze of old roads that offer hiking opportunities. A no-fee permit required. See Termination Point (page 156) for obtaining a permit.
U.S.G.S. Map:	Kodiak D-1.
Trail Begins:	At either end of island. Boat access.
Condition of Trail:	Old WWII roads.
Trail Facilities:	None.
Other Trail Users:	None.
Agency Contact:	Leisnoi Village Corporation. Phone: (907) 487-4929
Season of Use:	Summer/fall.
Safety Concerns:	Minimal. Watch weather patterns.

THREE SISTERS TRAIL (KO-10)
(Also called Pillar Mountain Trail)

Length (one way):	4.8 miles.
Trip Time (one way):	3 hours.
Degree of Difficulty:	Moderate.
Elevation Gain:	1,200 feet.
Unique Attractions:	Views of St. Paul Harbor, Chiniak Bay and Buskin River Valley.
Area Description:	Trail goes through thick alder and open meadowed country. It offers spectacular

	views and berry picking in season.
U.S.G.S. Map:	Kodiak D-2.
Trail Begins:	At end of the road on Pillar Mountain. Take Thorshem Street in downtown Kodiak to Poplar Avenue and turn left. This avenue turns into the Pillar Mountain Road.
Trail Ends:	Near the top of Three Sisters Mountain.
Condition of Trail:	Not maintained.
Trail Facilities:	None.
Other Trail Users:	An occasional four-wheeler.
Agency Contact:	Resource Management Officer Kodiak Island Borough 710 Mill Bay Road Kodiak, AK 99615 Phone: (907) 486-5736
Season of Use:	Summer/fall.
Safety Concerns:	Watch for the four-wheel-drive fans and keep an eye on the weather.

PYRAMID MOUNTAIN SOUTH (KO-11)

Length (one way):	1.5 miles.
Trip Time (one way):	1.5 hours.
Degree of Difficulty:	Moderate to difficult.
Elevation Gain:	2,200 feet.
Unique Attractions:	View of Buskin River Valley.
Area Description:	Moderately steep but open terrain offering excellent views.
U.S.G.S. Map:	Kodiak D-2.
Trail Begins:	Near the north end of Buskin Lake just west of a small creek.
Trail Ends:	In the alpine zone near Pyramid Mountain Peak.
Condition of Trail:	Not maintained.
Trail Facilities:	None.
Other Trail Users:	None.
Agency Contact:	Resource Management Office Kodiak Island Borough 710 Mill Bay Road Kodiak, AK 99615

Phone: (907) 486-5736
Season of Use: Summer/fall.
Safety Concerns: Steep terrain in some places.

PYRAMID MOUNTAIN NORTH (KO-12)

Length (one way):   1.9 miles.
Trip Time (one way):   1.5 hours.
Degree of Difficulty: Moderate to difficult.
Elevation Gain: 2,000 feet.
Unique Attractions: View of Buskin River Valley.
Area Description: Dense brushy vegetation with natural openings. More opportunity for distant viewing higher on the mountain. Some steep terrain on the upper slopes.
U.S.G.S. Map: Kodiak D-2.
Trail Begins: At parking lot near the pass on Anton Larson Bay, 3.3 miles beyond Buskin Lake and just beyond the old ski area.
Trail Ends: In the alpine zone, near Pyramid Mountain peak.
Condition of Trail: Not maintained.
Trail Facilities: Parking lot.
Other Trail Users: None.
Agency Contact: Resource Management Officer
                           Kodiak Island Borough
                           710 Mill Bay Road
                           Kodiak, AK 99615
                           Phone: (907) 486-5736
Season of Use: Summer/fall.
Safety Concerns: Minimal. Some steep terrain.

SKI SLOPE TRAIL (KO-13)

Length (one way):   1.2-1.5 miles.
Trip Time (one way):   1-1.2 hours.
Degree of Difficulty: Moderate to difficult.
Elevation Gain: 900 feet.
Unique Attractions: Excellent views of Anton Larsen Bay and Pyramid Mountain.

Area Description:	Brushy terrain with some good views.
U.S.G.S. Map:	Kodiak D-2.
Trail Begins:	At about Mile 3, just above the ski area.
Trail Ends:	On the ridge above ski area.
Condition of Trail:	Not maintained. May be wet and muddy.
Trail Facilities:	Minimal parking.
Other Trail Users:	Four-wheelers.
Agency Contact:	U.S. Coast Guard Station
	ATTN: Resource Management
	Kodiak, AK 99619
	Phone: (907) 487-5299
Season of Use:	Summer/fall.
Safety Concerns:	Minimal. An occasional brown bear.

CASCADE LAKE TRAIL (KO-14)

Length (one way):	2.5 miles.
Trip Time (one way):	1.9 hours.
Degree of Difficulty:	Moderate to difficult.
Elevation Gain:	400 feet.
Unique Attractions:	Access to Cascade Lakes and views of Anton Larsen Bay.
Area Description:	Trail crosses Red Cloud River, passes through coastal brushline and across three creeks, before dropping into the south end of Cascade Lake. Good fishing for rainbow trout.
U.S.G.S. Map:	Kodiak D-2.
Trail Begins:	About three-eighths of a mile before Anton Larson Bay. The last turn out before the Bay. Cross the creek and follow the edge of the Bay. You will see the trail rise up the ridge in front of you.
Trail Ends:	At Cascade Lake.
Condition of Trail:	Not maintained. Wet in spots.
Trail Facilities:	Minimal parking.
Other Trail Users:	None.
Agency Contact:	Ouzinkie Native Corp., P.O. Box 8 Ouzinkie, AK 99644
Season of Use:	Summer/fall.
Safety Concerns:	Hypothermia and brown bear.

BAROMETER MOUNTAIN (KO-15)

Length (one way):	1.9 miles.
Trip Time (one way):	1.5 hours.
Degree of Difficulty:	Difficult and steep.
Elevation Gain:	2,100 feet.
Unique Attractions:	Spectacular views of Kodiak, the Coast Guard Station and Chiniak Bay.
Area Description:	Trail goes through dense brush at lower elevations, rising sharply and becoming more open at the higher elevation. It follows the ridge line.
U.S.G.S. Map:	Kodiak D-2.
Trail Begins:	On a road west of the airport. As you go away from town, take the first road to the right immediately after the runway. Look for a well-worn trail on left.
Trail Ends:	Near top of Barometer Mountain.
Condition of Trail:	Not maintained.
Trail Facilities:	None.
Other Trail Users:	None.
Agency Contact:	U.S. Coast Guard Station (Trail open to public use.) ATTN: Resource Management Kodiak, AK 99619 Phone: (907) 487-5299
Season of Use:	Summer/fall.
Safety Concerns:	Avoid wet periods; very slick.

HEITMAN LAKE (KO-16)

Length (one way):	2 miles.
Trip Time (one way):	1.5 hours.
Degree of Difficulty:	Moderate to difficult.
Elevation Gain:	300 feet.
Unique Attractions:	Good fishing for rainbow trout.
Area Description:	The ridge country leading to the lake is a combination of Sitka spruce and cottonwood.
U.S.G.S. Map:	Kodiak C-2.
Trail Begins:	About two miles above Salonie Creek on

Chineak Bay Road. Look for small turnout on right. If you reach the dirt road leading to Cliff Point on Chineak Bay, you have gone a half-mile too far.

Trail Ends:	Heitman Lake.
Condition of Trail:	Not maintained, wet in spots.
Trail Facilities:	None.
Other Trail Users:	None.
Agency Contact:	Resource Management Officer
	Kodiak Island Borough
	710 Mill Bay Road
	Kodiak, AK 99615
	Phone: (907) 486-5736
Season of Use:	Summer/fall.
Safety Concerns:	Minimal. The lake water is extremely cold.

HEITMAN MOUNTAIN (KO-17)

Length (one way):	About 3 miles.
Trip Time (one way):	2 hours.
Degree of Difficulty:	Moderate to difficult.
Elevation Gain:	500 feet.
Unique Attractions:	Excellent views of Kodiak, the Coast Guard Base and Chiniak Bay.
Area Description:	The area offers a combination of Sitka spruce and cottonwood trees. At the end of the trail the vegetation turns to alders, with small scattered grassy meadows.
U.S.G.S. Map:	Kodiak C-2.
Trail Begins:	Just after a sharp turn in Chiniak Road as you approach Middle Bay. Slow down and look for a small turnout on the right. Once you can see Middle Bay on your left, you have gone too far.
Trail Ends:	On ridge below Heitman Mountain.
Condition of Trail:	Not maintained.
Trail Facilities:	None.
Other Trail Users:	None.
Agency Contact:	Resource Management Officer
	Kodiak Island Borough
	710 Mill Bay Road

Kodiak, AK 99615
Phone: (907) 486-5736

Season of Use:	Summer/fall.
Safety Concerns:	Minimal. Occasional brown bear. Watch for change in weather.

BROAD POINT LOOP TRAIL (KO-18)

Length (one way):	5.5 miles.
Trip Time (one way):	Can be broken into several short trips or one long one.
Degree of Difficulty:	Moderate.
Elevation Gain:	200 feet.
Unique Attractions:	Views of Middle and Kalsin bays and the rocky shoreline. Wildlife viewing is good, with deer, foxes, birds and seals.
Area Description:	This is lowland spruce forest with some mixed hardwoods. The coastline is rocky and rugged. A free permit is required. See Termination Point (page 156) for details.
U.S.G.S. Map:	Kodiak C-2
Trail Begins:	At the top of the switchback on Chiniak Road, near Mayflower Lake.
Trail Ends:	About a half-mile before Broad Point.
Condition of Trail:	Unmaintained.
Trail Facilities:	None.
Other Trail Users:	None.
Agency Contact:	Leisnoi Village Corporation Phone: (907) 487-4929
Season of Use:	Summer/fall.
Safety Concerns:	Steep rocky shoreline.

GULF OF ALASKA (KO-19)

Length (one way):	9 miles (about 4½ miles from each end to the Sacramento River).
Trip Time (one way):	6 hours.
Degree of Difficulty:	Moderate.
Elevation Gain:	Varies (never very steep).
Unique Attractions:	Views of the coastline along the Gulf of

Area Description:	The low rugged coastline is interspersed with some sandy beaches. You must find a suitable ford in order to cross the river (depends on recent rains). Try upstream. Contact the Burton Ranch (Bill or Kathy Burton, 907-486-3705) before driving the ranch roads to the trailhead.
U.S.G.S. Map:	Kodiak C-1, B-1, B-2.
Trail Begins:	At the old tracking station near Sequel Point. Take the Chiniak Road to Chiniak Point then continue by bearing right at the next two intersections.
Trail Ends:	Near the Burton Ranch Headquarters, which can be reached via the Pasagshak Road. Where the road continues to Narrow Cape, turn left on Kodiak Ranch Road. Close gates behind you.
Condition of Trail:	Not maintained.
Trail Facilities:	None.
Other Trail Users:	An occasional horse user on the Narrow Cape end.
Season of Use:	Summer/fall.
Safety Concerns:	Weather; crossing the Sacramento River. Brown bear have been reported. Avoid the Sequel Point Road during extremely wet weather.

NARROW CAPE (KO-20)

Length (one way):	4 miles.
Trip Time (one way):	2 hours.
Degree of Difficulty:	Easy to moderate.
Elevation Gain:	80 feet.
Unique Attractions:	The rugged Fossil Cliffs. Excellent bird-watching.
Area Description:	The trail starts at the end of the road at Narrow Cape, near Fossil Cliffs. It meanders to the beach, traverses Narrow Cape, loops between Twin Lakes and returns to the road about three-quarters of a mile from where it started.

U.S.G.S. Map:	Kodiak B-2.
Trail Begins:	Near the Loran Station, at the end of Narrow Cape Road. Turn right off Chiniak Road onto Pasagshak Bay Road and continue to Milepost 14.4. Turn right onto Narrow Cape Road to the end, about four miles.
Trail Ends:	About three-quarters of a mile back up the road from the trailhead.
Conditions of Trail:	Not maintained.
Trail Facilities:	None.
Other Trail Users:	None.
Agency Contact:	Alaska State Parks SR Box 3800 Kodiak, AK 99615 Phone: (907) 486-6339
Season of Use:	Summer/fall.
Safety Concerns:	Weather. Avoid the road during extremely wet weather.

SHUYAK ISLAND STATE PARK KAYAK SYSTEM (KO-21)

Length (one way):	Varies.
Trip Time (one way):	Varies.
Degree of Difficulty:	Easy to moderate.
Elevation Gain:	None.
Unique Attractions:	Rugged coastline, beaches, protected waterways and a great variety of marine mammals. Excellent fishing.
Area Description:	The 11,000-acre state park is located on the northwest part of the island. The island contains more sheltered interior waterways for the kayaker than anywhere in the Kodiak Archipelago, the best of which is contained within the state park. The land and sea offer excellent opportunities for birdwatching and wildlife viewing, with sightings of killer whales and Dall porpoises.

Kayaking Conditions:	Vary with tides and weather. Please contact Alaska State Parks for advice.
U.S.G.S. Map:	Afognak C-2, C-3.
Trail Begins:	Accessible by plane, it is 50 air miles from the city of Kodiak. Several Kodiak-based charter companies provide service to Shuyak Island. You must take a portable watercraft with you.
Trail Facilities:	Public-use cabins and portages (see map). Plus a roving ranger.
Other Trail Users:	An occasional motorized boat and commercial seine vessels.
Agency Contact:	Alaska State Parks SR Box 3800 Kodiak, AK 99615 Phone: (907) 486-6339
Season of Use:	Summer/fall.
Safety Concerns:	Weather is an extreme concern. Go waterproofed. Also, one may encounter an occasional brown bear.

CABINS

These are run by Alaska State Parks. Applications to:

Alaska State Parks
SR Box 3800
Kodiak, AK 99615
Phone: (907) 486-6339

SHUYAK ISLAND STATE PARK

Cabins are 12'x20' cedar, sleeping up to eight people. Fees are: December 1-May 31, $15/ per person per night (maximum of $30); June 1-November 30, $25/person per night (maximum of $50.) No refunds, except for emergency or administrative closures.

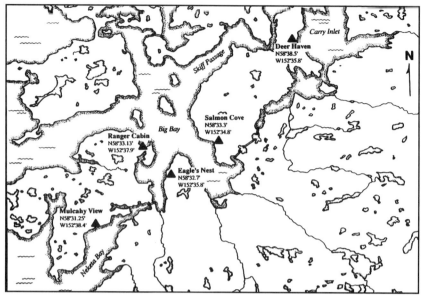

Map of Shuyak Island Public Use Cabins Alaska State Parks

CABIN REGULATIONS

Applications accepted up to 180 days in advance.
Stay is limited to seven days (a day runs from noon to noon).
Applicant must be 18 years or older.
The maximum size party is eight persons.
Reservations may be changed up to 10 days before booked date.
You must leave cabin in a clean and orderly condition.
Permits must be carried by holder at all times.

AFOGNAK ISLAND STATE PARK

Cabin regulations are essentially the same as those for Shuyak State Park, except the cost is $25/night.

The cabin is 12' x 14' and sleeps six people. It is located on Pillar Lake on the south end of Tanki Cape, Afognak Island.

➲   Both Shuyak State Park and Afognak State Park are accessible by boat or air charter out of the city of Kodiak.

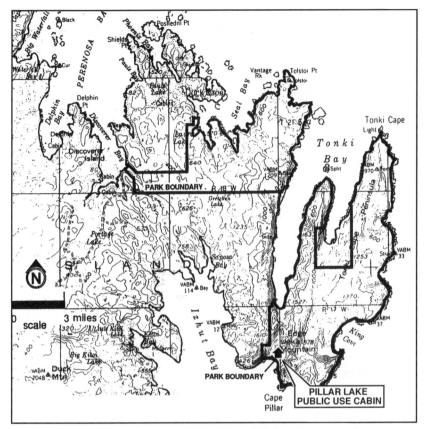

Map of Pillar Lake Cabins, Afognak Island State Park

KODIAK NATIONAL WILDLIFE REFUGE

All cabins are reserved through public drawings. Applications must be in prior to the drawing dates. Cabins not reserved by the drawing will be available on a first-come, first-served basis. Drawing dates are:

DATE OF DRAWING	FOR CABIN USE IN
January 2	April, May, June
April 1	July, August, September
July 1	October, November, December
October 1	January, February, March

Only one application per group will be accepted for a given cabin and specified dates. Names of group members must be on the application.

All refuge and state game and fish regulations must be adhered to. Applications should be addressed to:

Kodiak National Wildlife Refuge
1390 Buskin River Road
Kodiak, AK 99615
Phone: (907) 487-2600

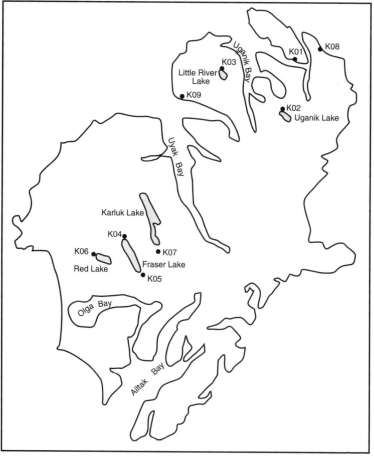

Map of Public Use Cabins Kodiak National Wildlife Refuge

Some portable watercraft may increase available recreational opportunities.

The fee is $20 per night. Do not send check or money order with applications. Fees are paid after the drawings. Failure to pay fee at least one month prior to departure will cancel your reservation.

CABIN REGULATIONS

All cabins must be left in a clean and orderly condition.
You must take your own fuel oil for heater, plus bring a cooking stove.

The following is a list of cabins, all of which are accessible only by boat or airplane:

KO1. Uganik Island – A 10x10-foot cabin with four bunks and an oil heater. Fishing is fair for Dolly Varden and pink salmon during summer and fall. Hunting for blacktail deer is good in early winter. Good marine estuaries and high alpine habitats for wildlife viewing and photography. U.S.G.S. Map: Kodiak D-4.

KO2. Uganik Lake – A 12x14-foot cabin with three bunks and an oil heater. Fishing is excellent for Dolly Varden and rainbow trout. Silver and red salmon fishing is available at the outlet of the lake and downstream. Hunting is good for brown bear and blacktail deer. Area offers excellent mountain vistas and wildlife photography. U.S.G.S. Map: Kodiak C-4.

KO3. Little River Lake – A 10x12-foot cabin with four bunks and an oil heater. Pink, silver and red salmon fishing is fair at the lake outlet. Dolly Varden and rainbow trout are available in the lake and nearby streams during the summer. Bear hunting is good. Early season deer hunting is good. Use of cabin after November 1 is discouraged due to lake freeze-up. U.S.G.S. Map: Kodiak D-5.

KO4. North Frazer Lake – A 10x12-foot cabin with four bunks and an oil heater. Fishing is good for Dolly Varden, rainbow trout and red salmon. Hunting for brown bear is good; deer, poor. Use of this cabin after November 1 is discouraged due to lake freeze-up. U.S.G.S. Quad Map: Karluk B-1, Alaska.

KO5. South Frazer Lake – A 12x20-foot cabin with six bunks and a wood stove. Fishing for steelhead, chum, pink and red salmon in the Dog Salmon River can be outstanding, but may require considerable hiking. Brown bear hunting is good; early season blacktail deer hunting is also popular. Many wildlife viewing and photography opportunities. Use of this cabin after November 1 is discouraged due to lake freeze-up. U.S.G.S. Map: Karluk A-1.

KO6. Viekoda Bay – A 10x12-foot cabin with four bunks and an oil stove. Fishing is fair for pink salmon. Deer hunting is good in fall/early winter. Brown bear and duck hunting is fair. Marine estuaries and alpine habitats offer a variety of bird and wildlife viewing.

KO7. Blue Fox Bay – A 10x20-foot cabin with four bunks and an oil heater. Fishing is fair to good for silver salmon during August and September. Hunting for brown bear or deer is fair. Excellent wildlife viewing in a scenic spruce coastal environment. U.S.G.S. Map: Afognak B-3. **Note:** Cabin is on Afognak Island and not shown on the map.